The Human Experience is the Dance of Heaven and Earth

A Call Home to Peace

Dhyana Stanley

BOOKS

Winchester, UK
Washington, USA

First published by O-Books, 2016
O-Books is an imprint of John Hunt Publishing Ltd., Laurel House, Station Approach,
Alresford, Hants, SO24 9JH, UK
office1@jhpbooks.net
www.johnhuntpublishing.com

For distributor details and how to order please visit the 'Ordering' section on our website.

ISBN: 978 1 78535 340 6
Library of Congress Control Number: 2015958987

A CIP catalogue record for this book is available from the British Library.

Design: Stuart Davies

Printed and bound by CPI Group (UK) Ltd, Croydon, CR0 4YY, UK

The Human Experience is the Dance of Heaven and Earth

A Call Home to Peace

CONTENTS

To all those
who go within
with fresh eyes.

If your eye be single, your whole body will be full of light.

—Jesus

The real voyage of discovery consists not in seeking new landscapes, but in having new eyes.

—Marcel Proust

The direct perception is ever-present Experience.

—Ramana Maharshi

Chapter 1

The Journey Out of All That Seems So Personal

The Suffering and Search

Just about everyone at one time or another has had the sense that there has to be more to life than what we currently know. There is a feeling that there has to be another way of living—that stress, restlessness, conflict, fear and war are just not natural. Stressful living doesn't feel natural and free, and there is something undeniable within that propels us to discover our natural state of unconditional peace and freedom.

My own sense of inner conflict was very intense even as a young child. Something didn't seem quite right and nothing really felt like home, not the family I grew up with, my physical surroundings, or even my own skin. It wasn't that the family I grew up with was awful—it was as if there was something inside me that felt alien to my surroundings. But because others seemed to fit in just fine, I came to deeply believe that there is something wrong with me.

As I grew into my teens I began to feel that there had to be another way of being in this world than what I was experiencing so, because I often felt a pull toward God, I tried religion. And for a time I did experience a level of peace, but it was conditional and limited to just certain areas of life. This peace did not transfer into the entirety of everyday life and did not last, and I knew that truth would, so for quite a while I thought the answer was in deepening my beliefs. So I studied more, prayed more, attended more meetings, and married a man who like me was heading to Mexico to serve as a missionary. But although we were missionaries and raising our children in the faith there continued to be an almost constant restlessness or dissatisfaction with life, which registered as a feeling that something is missing and I began to feel like a hypocrite.

And then everything came to a head when I watched the movie *Gandhi* while we were in Texas renewing our visas. As I saw this Hindu man actually embody Jesus' teachings and live all aspects of life with such peace, love and an absence of fear I came away from that movie deeply disturbed.

How could this man be condemned to hell? According to my beliefs he was going to hell and it just did not seem to be the truth. And I also came away from that movie more profoundly disturbed about my own experience. Here I was a Christian missionary yet my daily experience of life did not line up with Jesus' teaching. It seemed to me that the core of his teaching is that the kingdom of heaven is within and it is here and now—yet this life of unconditional peace, love and fearlessness Jesus spoke of and lived was certainly not my experience.

But it was all too disturbing to look at any deeper so I tried to bury my questions. And for a while it seemed to work until I began to have anxiety attacks and then went into a deep depression. But thankfully, I did not believe those symptoms had to do with the body or some medical or hormonal issue, but felt they had some emotional basis. So I then looked deeper than the physical. And as I looked at what I was experiencing, I became a bit more honest about what I was pushing away and gradually the connection between my physical symptoms and my dishonesty became very clear; I saw my health improve the more honest I became. As I no longer resisted what now felt truest (that I no longer believed certain things), the anxiety attacks stopped and I slowly came out of the depression and that was the very beginning of a deepening commitment to honesty, no matter the cost.

This process of becoming more honest and clear about my current level of experience, however, actually took many years. We were back living in the United States when I finally saw that I was either going to live a lie or tell my family that I would no longer be attending church with them. The children were old enough to understand what was going on as well as to express fear for my soul but I knew I could no longer move in opposition to what I knew to be true so I told my family why I would no longer be attending church.

But even with this level of honesty, there was still a nagging, persistent, almost constant sense of lack or that something is wrong. Something seemed off but I had no idea what it was so for many years I bounced between believing that if life would just line up the way I thought it should then I would finally be at peace, to believing that nothing external needed to change but that I just needed to change.

During those rare times when externals lined up the way I wanted, peace was experienced but it never lasted very long at all before I felt something else is now needed, and the sense of lack and restlessness slipped back in.

And throughout the internal searching and attempts to fix myself, there was the deep belief that my mind was certainly capable, with God's help of course, to find the missing key and unlock the secret. Because I previously mistook my ability to figure out the connection between my dishonesty and ill health as what caused the health to return, I then believed that the answer lies in my rational mind. It wasn't until many years later when I realized that there was nothing that needed to be figured out—that it was the rejection of the current level of truth (that I no longer held certain beliefs) that contributed to the ill health, and it was the acceptance of the current level of truth that allowed the healing. Whether I ever saw or figured out that the dishonesty contributed to the ill health didn't matter in the least. My health was already returning with the simple acceptance of the current level of truth. It was only in retrospect that the connection between my level of honesty and health became clear. (All of this is not to say that dishonesty underlies all medical conditions, but only that it is very helpful to see all challenges, health issues included, as opportunities for deeper insights or more fully relaxing into what is discovered beyond the physical.)

But because I didn't see any of that at the time I thought I was being honest by using my mind to try and figure out what is true, so for many years then I relied solely on my ability to think. I believed that if I could just figure out what it is about my past that caused this flaw, which continued to bring up the feeling that something is missing, then all would be well. So over the years, I filled ten and a half inches of stacked journals with attempts to figure it all out, but nothing really worked.

And because of all this internal analysis, I became increasingly more aware of the dysfunctional aspects of my personality, and how they played out in daily life and created all kinds of conflict. The relationship with two of my three adult children suffered as they reacted (thankfully) to my subtle and what I initially considered loving attempts to 'help'. I came to see it all clearly and eventually took complete responsibility for my controlling behavior, yet was utterly powerless to do anything about it. It was as if I was literally possessed to do and say certain things even though I sometimes clearly saw beforehand how dysfunctional it was. It was hell on earth to be aware of that all and not be able to do a thing about it.

So deepening beliefs did not work and then changing beliefs to either the belief that the external world needed to change or the belief that I needed to change did not work, and as the years went on the desperation grew.

And then thankfully something happened which resulted in a lot of suffering and utter confusion about life, and I went within exclusively. There was no more bouncing back and forth between trying to find the answer externally and then going within. There were no more periods of blaming anything or anyone. I took sole responsibility for my internal state. There was now an all-consuming urge that arose to find the truth and I knew it had to be within.

But this time when I went within it was largely without the personal agenda of trying to fix myself. This suffering and confusion was bigger than anything I had experienced before, and there was a profound urge to find the truth about life rather than fix me. And after I was able to forgive the one who I believed had hurt me, somehow I came to sense that if I wanted to find the truth I should honor what I now know as the truest. And honoring what I then knew as the truest seemed the same as honoring my heart or what now feels most joyful. To consciously honor my joy felt the same as honoring what now feels truest or most authentic—not in order to reach some personal goal but simply for the sake of truth.

So when the inclination came to have all the neighbors on the block over for a gathering and that appealed to me, then I consciously followed through, even though this was somewhat outside my personality's comfort zone. And when the inclination came to become involved in an activist organization and that appealed to me, even though this was something far outside of my personality's comfort zone, then I consciously followed through.

Although I didn't realize it at the time, this search of going within by saying yes to what now seems truest opened up a very different level of seeking. Previous searching within had a personal agenda because it ignored joy or what now seems truest and kept me focused on resisting life and trying to fix what I believed needed fixing.

But although this honoring of joy seemed the truest in the moment, the deeper search for truth was always there in the background. Even though I began to feel better as the intense suffering lessened, my search for truth did not lessen in the least. The urge to find out what is true was all consuming. I deeply felt that there had to be a universal truth, it had to be beyond culture, it had to be permanent and it had to transfer into all areas of life or life made no sense at all and there was no way out of suffering.

The Realization

And then some time after this earnest honoring of whatever the heart prompted, I came across the book *A New Earth* by the spiritual teacher Eckhart Tolle and everything shifted. During the first reading I sensed there is something very profound that he is pointing to but I didn't know what it was, so when I was internally prompted to reread it I consciously followed through. And it was during the second reading when there was a deep twofold realization. I realized that I am whole already and that my mind has nothing to do with this realization.

The realization that I am whole already—that who I truly am, whatever that is, is not flawed or lacking anything—went deep. That realization permeated my whole being and was permanent even though there was a lot of forgetfulness. Even with forgetfulness I knew that only the sensing of Wholeness was temporarily obscured but Wholeness itself is not missing. There was profound clarity that what I truly am is eternally whole and does not in any way whatsoever need to be healed, fixed, transformed or to evolve. The realization and expression of who I am gradually integrated or evolved, and continues to evolve or deepen, but the essence of who I am does not evolve.

I also realized that my rational mind not only had nothing to do with this realization but that it actually got in the way. It was initially startling to see that that very thing which I had trusted to free me was the very thing that kept me enslaved. Because I mistakenly believed my body was healed of the anxiety attacks by my mind's ability to figure out what is true, rather than the actual acceptance of the current level of truth itself, for many years I trusted fully in my mind's ability to find the answer. And even though it consistently did not work, I never stopped to consider that my mind may be the very thing that is preventing the answer from being realized.

When Wholeness was realized the whole foundation for what I thought I was shifted out from under me. There is nothing wrong with me, there is nothing to fix, and this crazy, negative talking chatter within is not true. It literally felt as if an enormous weight had been lifted off my shoulders and a deep stillness and peace arose. It truly finally felt like Home.

Integration of the Realization Within

I can't say, however, that it was all smooth sailing from that point on. For quite some time I still continued to seek for who I am. It was a profound realization of wholeness yet only a glimpse into who I truly am. Although I knew I am not in need of fixing and I knew I am not my mind, I had very little sense of who I am. Although I knew that whatever I am is whole there was a lot of forgetfulness during the day, continued negative emotions and negative patterns of behavior and only brief glimpses of the sense of wholeness. But even in all of that I knew wholeness and peace as truth and as ever present. I knew without a doubt that during the times of forgetfulness truth is not absent—only the sensing of truth or peace is temporarily obscured. And because I knew peace as the ever-present truth, I was very earnest not only in the sensing of it but also in clearly seeing what is obscuring it during those times of forgetfulness.

This open sensing of peace and the clear seeing through of what is obscuring it was a deeper honoring of joy or truth because I now directly knew Wholeness as permanent, ever-present truth. And because I knew truth would affect all areas of life—not only at the level of my understanding but also at the level of what I now sense and how I now express myself—I was very earnest in the honoring or confirming of what is true at all levels of my experience.

So whenever I became aware of negative emotions I knew that they were the only thing obscuring the sense of peace, so I was interested in looking closely at them. And gradually, I saw that all negative emotions have the same signature feel that something is lacking or wrong, and that my sense of well-being is dependent on something being different now, in this moment. And because I knew that my true sense of self, the sense of well-being, is not dependent on anything I looked at what I was now believing it to be dependent on—which I saw is the same as looking at what I am now believing to be lacking. And every time I looked at what I believed was lacking, I saw clearly that it is not true. Consistently, I saw that there is nothing lacking—that the sense of well-being is full now.

It became very clear that negative emotions point back to a belief, a specific belief about how something more is needed to sense peace, and when questioned I saw directly that it is completely false. I saw that it is only what I happen to believe about life now that is creating the untrue impression that something is wrong. With absolute consistency I observed that when the belief in lack is seen all the way through the sense of lack dissolves and peace is sensed.

Gradually, I realized that the question 'What is true?' is another way to ask 'Who am I?'. I saw that the question 'Do I now need anything to be different to sense well-being?' is another way to ask 'Do I now need anything to be different to sense and recognize who I actually am?'. That question, 'Do I now need anything to be different to sense well-being', was like a precision laser beam cutting through all that is untrue and laying bare what is eternally here.

And gradually, another aspect of experience also came into focus. I saw that whenever I judged how life is now showing up not only did life feel as if it is lacking but so did I. I saw directly how all judgments, even of the weather, obscured not only the true sense of life but that of my true nature. And I observed that when life is experienced directly, absent of all judgments, there is no sense of lack in life or self.

The connection between life and self then became very clear, and what I saw as beliefs began to include all judgments. Initially, I only questioned beliefs I had about myself but gradually saw how beliefs are really just any judgments about now.

Again and again I consistently observed how my true sense of well-being was only being obscured by whatever I happened to believe. It became clear that it is only belief that is creating the false sense of lack—not thought. I observed directly how thoughts passing through freely do not alter the sense of peace, but the very instant I identify with them they do. I began to see that it is only from the position of peace that peace is sensed—when I grabbed hold of thoughts life felt very different than when I allowed them to move freely.

I then saw that at each moment I am free to experience life as it is believed to be and then feel as if life and I am lacking; and I am free to experience life directly as it actually is and sense peace internally and externally. The contrast between belief and direct experience was becoming very clear.

Earnestly then, from the moment I woke up to the moment I went to sleep, my sole purpose was truth. My attention was now one-pointed—to sense my natural state of peace and during times of forgetfulness to see through what I had mistakenly believed I needed for a sense of well-being back into the true sense of reality. Not back to reality as if there is ever an actual leaving of reality, but more like back into the conscious direct sense or recognition of reality. And as I continued to inquire into truth and confirm the sensing of it, I saw how my mind is now working in service to truth, and eventually came to realize that it is not 'my' mind at all.

Gradually, the sense of stillness and peace deepened and the periods of remembering increased. But even with an increased sense of stillness and peace, I continued to react unconsciously as intense negative reactive patterns continued to play out for quite some time. Even though it was clear that they are not who I truly am, I still had some confusion and even despair around why they were continuing so strongly for so long.

The deepening sense of inner peace was fine but if I am not free to respond in love and actually express peace, even to those closest to me, I knew it could not be the truth and I wanted nothing to do with it. I knew truth would transfer into every aspect of daily life without exception. And even though the quality of this peace seemed very different than the quality of peace that had been experienced when I had certain religious beliefs, I had to be sure it transferred into the entirety of life before I would fully trust it. So for a time, at one level, I was testing whatever this is to make sure it is true within the totality of my experience and yet at a deeper level I knew it as truth so I earnestly continued on. Thankfully, Life honored my deepest intention for truth alone.

And although during this period I periodically thought that a mystical experience is needed to blast all conditioning out of my system and plunge me into some altered blissful state, I thankfully did not wait for that. There was no waiting at all. That thought, without belief, did not alter the one-pointed openness to life now. There was only a steady earnest focused openness to sense what actually is now, and a trust that maybe there actually is some process to all of this after all. Gradually, this earnest openness revealed the absolute power of Now and all feeling of needing a mystical experience eventually dissolved naturally.

But during this period as these negative reactive patterns repeatedly took hold again and again, I remained interested in only what actually is. As I observed and contemplated my experience in light of wholeness, which I knew to be true, I saw that these intense negative reactive patterns don't seem to come directly from beliefs like other negative emotions do. These emotional patterns come up suddenly and then go into thought—

not the other way around. And gradually, I became aware of three things: that these negative patterns are coming up to be 'felt or experienced through' (unlike beliefs and the emotions that follow which come up to be 'seen through'), that Life is actually creating the opportunities for all beliefs and emotional patterns to come up in order to be set free, and also, that regardless of how often the same emotional pattern or belief comes up it is now that they are to be experienced or seen through.

Regardless of how many times those patterns showed up, I came to understand that it is the fresh experiencing of what actually is now where life and power is. The clear 'seeing and experiencing through' of the belief or emotional pattern an hour ago does not transfer over to now. Life does not acknowledge a 'ditto that' attitude.

And also, I came to see that everything, even trapped feelings, wants to be in its natural state. So these negative emotional patterns are coming up to be set free—to finally be experienced as they actually are. And just as unattached, passing thoughts do not alter the true sense of wholeness, so it is with unattached, passing feelings. When experienced purely, as they actually are, feelings do not have any sense of lack about them but the very instant I identified with them they certainly seemed to. I consistently saw that it is only from my true position of peace that peace is revealed—when I grabbed hold of feelings life felt very different than when I allowed them to move freely.

And because I consistently observed that it is solely beliefs and emotions, not thoughts and feelings, which project an untrue impression that I need something for a sense of wellbeing—whenever beliefs and emotions were experienced I saw how significant it is to set all thoughts and feelings free. And when I saw that, it gradually became very clear that life is actually, literally shaping itself in service to this setting free.

I observed how negative emotions and emotional patterns only come up as life takes certain shapes. Only when certain things happened did I judge life and then falsely feel as if something needed to change for a sense of well-being, which then allowed the opportunity to question that misperception. I realized that this peace that we all are is so radical that it includes the totality—so if a certain look or word or string of words from another or any thought, feeling or event at all throws us, then life will lovingly shape itself as that exact thought, look or event in order for us to realize unconditional peace now.

This understanding opened up a whole different dimension of experience. I realized that life now is shaping itself in service to peace because if I can only sense the truth of who I am when life only takes very limited shapes, then I am not truly free. A thought, a feeling, rain, a painful tooth, the passing of a loved one, an illness—I realized that all of it is Love itself pointing the way to peace. No exceptions.

Life, then, became my Teacher. Life was trusted and opened to, regardless of what form it took. I trusted that however life is showing up right now is always in direct service to truth. As I simply remained open to the totality of life and allowed all thoughts and feelings as they actually are, those persistent negative emotional patterns loosened and transmuted into what they truly are which allowed a more stable sense of who I am.

With the dissolving of conditioned patterns, there was a gradual inner integration of what I know to be true with what I now sense. There was much more internal harmony between what I directly understand with what I now sense. Initially, there was often a disconnect or disharmony between what I experientially know and what I now sense, but gradually that inner disconnect dissolved. With the dissolving of conditioned patterns, there was much more of an integrated, stable unconditional natural sense of inner harmony which allowed some, but not yet full, freedom of expression.

Integration of the Realization Within the Whole of Life

Even though there was a deepening sense of who I am which, at one level, gave way to a profound, stable understanding that I am one with life—a feeling of separation in certain areas of life continued. At the experiential level, there was still a feeling of separation between the internal and external.

Life itself seemed fragmented, frightening in certain areas and safe in others, which at one level I knew was not the truth. Although I knew life and self not to be separate and there was therefore nothing to fear, there was not yet an integration of this knowing at the level of sensing this within the whole of life, and because I knew truth would affect all areas of life I knew the realization was not yet full.

I knew that in order for life or self to more fully express itself through my human form there has to be an integration between understanding and sensing the internal and external as not separate. I observed again and again how fear of life, or the seemingly external expressions of life, does not allow me to respond lovingly. My body still, at some level, felt separate from the whole of life. Although I knew that I am whole, it felt as if this wholeness that I am was exclusively contained within my body, so a sense of separation and fear of life kept coming up. The true universal body was not yet sensed.

So I sent out a heartfelt YES to whatever is needed—that no matter what, I want to realize the full truth of who I am. And it was soon after that Yes that several unusual challenging events took place, which were accepted, and then it was as if my whole being shifted energetically and it literally felt as if I no longer fit in certain places. And at just the perfect moment, in the very midst of this shift, Life brought me to the teaching of Adyashanti.

Although I've never been in his physical presence, his words, "We are all dancing a dance—dance yours all the way through," and the energy within them carried a steadiness and profound resolve that went directly to my heart and came back to me often during the challenges ahead. His teachings, during this period, were instrumental in pointing the way to a deeper surrender or allowing of however life is moving. Gradually, I realized that allowing how life is now expressing itself not only within but through the body is part of what cooperation with the dance of the whole involves.

The allowing of life now was deepening from an internal level of allowing thoughts and feelings to be in their unconditioned state, to an external level of allowing the body to be and move in its unconditioned state. And I noticed that the deeper the allowing of how life is now flowing, regardless of where it took me, the less frightening, fragmented and separate life seemed and the boundaries of internal and external began to dissolve.

So when it became clear that life was moving me to make a major change that was far outside my conditioning—I did willingly. This is not to say that waves of sadness and fear did not periodically come up, but those feelings did not cause any lasting resistance to move with truth. And the initial resistance that did come along with intense suffering and then willing movement all served to deepen the sense of love—as well as the steadiness of movement regardless of where life was bringing me, so to speak.

After that movement was willingly made this immense sense of Love arose. This love for only That Which Is took hold and filled my being. This love included everything, even more challenges that came. So when it was clear some time later that there was another major change to be made, it was made willingly. On the tail of making that change, however, certain things happened, intense fears came up along with continued willing movement even in the midst of those fears and then life brought me to be in the physical presence of the spiritual teacher, Francis Lucille.

The impact of the weeklong retreat with Francis is hard to explain in words but over the months following it there was an increased sense of the potency of that meeting. There was a very gradual dissolving of notions I had about how an awakened being would be, along with notions of how the true sense of presence would feel. Ideas about perfection of expression and extraordinary bliss faded, and there was a deeper relaxation into and as Life.

Although it may seem unnecessarily excessive to go into such detail about my own journey, the intention for this is to bring to light the common threads that run through all of our journeys—and to dispel the myth that a mystical experience is required. The surface particulars vary from person to person but what keeps us stuck and what opens us up, so to speak, don't.

Being aware of some of those common threads within the journey of all seekers, as well as the 'journey' after the glimpse of Stillness, can be extremely helpful.

We are all in this human experience together—literally.

Chapter 2

The Unfolding of the Discovery

The Search

There is most definitely another way of living and relating than what most humans know, but each one of us must directly discover this for ourself. It is of no real use to read this or any other spiritual book in order to learn about peace or about who you are—but it is of profound use if for one moment you are open enough to discover firsthand whether what is pointed to within these pages is true or not. Not to try and verify what you believe—that you are either flawed or whole or that peace is absent or is present—but to discover now, in this moment, what actually is when nothing is believed.

When we don't know who we are there is something deep within that feels as if we are living a lie. If we did not feel as if we were living a lie we would all be satisfied with our experience now and would not seek the reality of who we are. Dissatisfaction is proof of untruth because there is something embedded in our DNA that knows what is true feels natural and free.

But although the human experience for most is largely dissatisfying, we don't realize who we are when we try to retreat from it but when we finally experience it as it truly is. We don't realize who we are in spite of the human experience but within it fully.

When we are in deep sleep we don't experience this human dimension of form, and when we are in deep sleep we don't come to realize who we are. It is only in the waking state within the conscious, direct experience of form that we wake up to the reality of who we are.

The Form Life is Now Taking is Pointing to Truth

All true teaching points to our formless essence, but sometimes the teaching is without a lot of pointing to the direct experience of form. Because form is often mistakenly interpreted as having personal meaning and no form has personal meaning or purpose, sometimes the true teaching points away from form directly to the formless. This pointing is very valuable for those who can hear it, but for those who can't there is another direct pointing.

The pointing within the teaching written here states that within the human dimension everything has meaning or purpose—not personal meaning but universal meaning in service of the dissolving of all that seems so personal. This pointing, therefore, points directly through form (as it actually is, neither personal nor separate) to the formless. All form or however life now shows up is in service to truth.

Although at one level the pointing within the two forms of the same teaching may seem contradictory, at a deeper level they are not at all. All seeming contradiction falls away when reality is realized.

When we directly experience Life now as it actually is, which includes the form it is taking—this is the true experience of Self. Regardless of whether the teaching primarily points to the true experience or the true experiencer, it does not matter in the least.

When all is experienced as it truly is, nothing is believed or felt to be either personal or separate, and the true experience and experiencer come into focus and are gradually realized as one. Life and Self are realized as one.

The question 'Who or what am I?' is another way to ask 'What is true right now?' or 'What is the true experience of Now or of Life?'. And the true experience of life now, within the human dimension, does not exclude form.

There is no real separation between spirit and matter, mind or consciousness and the body, the invisible and visible, the formless and form, heaven and earth. The realization of who we are is the realization that all already is heaven here on earth. 'On earth as it is in heaven' is the discovery of who we already are. Heaven and earth only seem separate when we identify exclusively with form.

So if life shows up as an irate driver who cuts us off and we are open to discover what is true right now—this is the openness to discover who we are. There is no need to rush home in order to quiet ourself by meditating or praying. The discovery is always now, in the very midst of daily life and thoughts and feelings.

Earth is our classroom and Life is our teacher, but the classroom and teacher are anything but traditional.

Earth is not a traditional classroom where we attend for several hours a day, and then go and live the rest of our life. The entirety of our human experience is the classroom not just when we are praying or meditating, but also when we are paying our bills and changing diapers and stuck in traffic and burying a loved one and aware of a judgmental thought passing through.

In this Earth School, nothing needs to be learned and no accumulation of knowledge or technique is required. In this school, unlike others, it is the firsthand discovery of life now, unfiltered by accumulated knowledge, that is pointed to. Unlike book knowledge, this discovery is only made when the belief that more of anything is needed, knowledge included, is dropped for just a moment. Only then do we have 'eyes that see' what is fully, completely already now.

This classroom gives us complete freedom to discover truth now or remain unconscious of truth. We are free to believe thoughts that life now is lacking and then feel as if we are lacking and then act that out and contribute to others' false sense of lack, and we are free to be free of that all and realize directly the falsity of lack.

And the true teacher—Life—is also anything but traditional. She is not a strict taskmaster, handing us books and tests to learn and pass. Literally, she is love taking the shape of the car that won't start or the belief that life is frightening or the emotion of anger about life being unfair. This Teacher is love itself manifesting as whatever is showing up right now in our daily life reflecting back exactly what we are now taking ourself to be. When we believe that we are lacking and separate, life then lovingly reflects that unreality back to us as a feeling of discontent.

Just as the physical body is lovingly designed to register physical pain when something happens to jolt it out of its natural relaxed state—so it is with the mind. Within this human dimension, consciousness or mind has a kind of fluidity to it. We can actually misperceive the reality of who we are, which then thankfully registers as discontent. Whenever we, consciousness, identify with the contents within consciousness, our thoughts and feelings, we feel the dissatisfying unnaturalness of that misidentification.

The Feelings of Internal and External Dissolve

With a few rare humans the discovery of who we are may be realized and integrated in its entirety within the first glimpse of truth, but for most of us that is not the case. Most of us will initially glimpse our true nature and then when known to be permanent, even with forgetfulness, there is a flushing up and dissolving of conditioned patterns. With this dissolving of conditioned patterns comes a more integrated sense of our essence, which gives way to a stable remembrance regardless of any thought or feeling that may ripple through. This internal harmony between what is directly known and what is sensed allows an increased sensitivity to life's flow. And as we are willing to move with life's flow, this willing movement gives way to the integrated realization of being within and as the whole of Life and the feelings of inner and outer dissolve.

Some may have very light conditioning that is flushed up in order to be experienced through and others of us may have very dense conditioning that is flushed up in order to be experienced through, but this process of setting free everything that has been frozen in time or unreality is all part of the deepening discovery. Resisting this flushing up and setting free of conditioning is resistance to the integration of the realization into all aspects of our human experience—understanding, sensing and expressing. Although this human experience is not who we essentially are, it is actually 'the way in' to fully realizing what is independent of this human experience.

When the mind is in its natural state, which is to say that Universal Mind or Consciousness is realized, the body gradually follows—if we are willing. When the conditioned sense of self is seen through then conditioned ways of moving in this world begin to feel alien. Movements motivated by the sense of lack or fear now feel very unnatural, and an increased sensitivity to life's flow reveals itself.

We sense life now moving in unconditioned ways often first in minor areas of daily life and then possibly in more major areas. As we cooperate and move with the unconditioned whole, regardless of how far outside our conditioning that movement may be, love reveals itself, a deeper trust takes hold and gradually all sense of borders and limits dissolves as well as fear. Life then ceases to seem separate and fragmented, and the unwavering trust gives way to a full integrated sense of our true universal body—Life itself.

That Which is Whole is Whole—Lack and Separation are Not Real

That which is universal is whole and unified so the integrated discovery of our universal nature is the full dissolving of the sense of lack and separation or the personal—as well as what projects from that. If lack is unfounded then so is desire and if separation is unfounded then so is fear. And if desire and fear are unfounded then so are attempts to control. As calculating, controlling and fear-based reactions fall away a much more natural, spontaneous and loving way of being shows itself.

This is not to say, however, that after the stabilization of the realization there are no desires, but these desires are not from a sense of lack but from a sense of joy and love to express what already is. These desires are not needs but are the heart's desire to express and celebrate and explore life.

When unified wholeness is realized this is the discovery that desire from the sense of lack and fear have no validity. If all is well now, if there is truly a sense of well-being now, then nothing more is needed and there is nothing that is feared. There is no desire not because desire is being denied, but because there is the recognition of fulfillment of all desire. In the direct recognition of reality, desire for something more or different just does not arise.

We are home in the heart of our being, and when home it is realized that nothing is missing. And as we settle into this space of no lack, so to speak, we also gradually realize the truth of no separation. Initially, the sense of wholeness may feel as if it is more localized or personal rather than universal, but for those who remain open all will be made clear. As fear is consciously experienced and moved through, it dissolves, and with the dissolving of fear the recognized sense of our universality is revealed. We know and sense directly the truth of no separation, and then life is no longer feared.

The process of the integration of the discovery then involves the clear seeing through of any residual desire or sense of lack and the pure experiencing through of any residual fear or sense of separation that causes forgetfulness. And although it may not initially register that seeing through the sense of lack, as well as fear, is actually a seeing through of the imagined personal self this truth will gradually reveal itself as you remain open to what actually is. As the feelings of lack and separation dissolve so does the feeling of a personal consciousness—universal consciousness is revealed as the essence of our individual, yet not separate, expression.

When a thought is believed and then something is felt to be needed for a sense of well-being, the light of clear seeing clears up all misperception. And when a feeling is personalized and then something feared or felt needs to be different for a sense of well-being, the light of pure experiencing clears up all misperception. Gradually, there is a depth of freedom realized that allows all thoughts and feelings to come and go freely without any effect whatsoever on our true sense of well-being—and without any altering of unconditioned movements. The mind and body, the formless and form, in their natural state are now consciously resting in and as the Whole.

When all residual desire and fear fall away so does the attempt to control, which is a conditioned reactive response to the feeling that 'I need something more or different'. When we feel something is missing we then try to control life to get what we believe is missing—we are not free to respond outside our conditioning. But when we realize that there is nothing missing then there is absolutely nothing that we feel needs to be controlled. All is allowed to be as it actually is. When this is realized, however, it does not mean that we no longer respond to situations, but that responses that come come from true understanding and love rather than misperception and fear.

Feelings of Time (Lack) and Space (Separation) Dissolve

This all unfolds naturally when we, from our true position of wholeness, allow all thoughts and feelings to flow freely. The beliefs in psychological time and personal space that hold together a false, personal sense of self dissolve to reveal the essence of being so open that it is without the chains of time or boundaries.

The integration of the realization of our timeless, universal nature dissolves both the beliefs and feelings of a personal self located within the limits of time and space. When desires dissolve so does the belief in psychological time, and when fear dissolves so does the belief in personal space. Although the concepts of time and space continue for practical purposes, we realize that no time is needed for a complete sense of well-being and that the whole of Life now is our home.

This dissolving of the beliefs and feelings of time and space happens naturally and there may not even be any conceptual understanding that this is what is unfolding, which is perfectly fine. There is no need to understand this or anything conceptually. Conceptual understanding of reality being outside of time and space does not create the sensing of reality. And having no conceptual understanding of our true nature being outside of those concepts does not obscure the sensing of it. When we realize who we are, unified wholeness is our conscious experience and regardless of whether our universal nature is conceptually understood to be outside of psychological time and personal space, it is.

The direct discovery of our universal nature is the direct discovery that lack and separation, a personal self, are not reality. And although there is often first a glimpse or realization of our natural mind or that lack is not real, this is not always the case. There may first be a glimpse of our natural body or that separation is not real. But regardless of how the realization initially registers it often moves or deepens as a spiral rather than sequentially. If we initially glimpse our natural mind there is often a deepening clarity and sensing of truth beyond the conditioned sense of lack, a relaxing into and moving with life beyond the conditioned sense of separation or fear, into a deepening clarity and sensing of truth at the level of the unconditioned natural mind into more natural, spontaneous movement at the level of the unconditioned body.

Some Main Pointers

This book addresses the unfolding at both of those levels of our human experience within two sections, but within each section there are three main pointers.

The first pointer is that awakening is a discovery—not a teaching. It is experiential, not conceptual. The realization and integration of that realization is an ever-deepening discovery of that which is already now.

Although teachings may be very helpful in pointing to truth, it is only the firsthand discovery of truth that impacts our experience. If we study or learn a particular teaching, that knowledge will not impact who we experientially know ourself to be or the way we express who we are. We must directly discover for ourself the truth of who we are at all levels of this human experience.

The second main pointer is that however life is now showing up is exactly what is in service to this discovery. All of life is moving to wake us up to who we already are.

Within our waking state life is becoming conscious of what it already is, which is to say that we are becoming conscious of what we already are. And whatever form life takes now is in service to this awakening—no exceptions. Everything, absolutely everything, that happens in our daily lives, from what is considered the smallest to the biggest, the most negative to the most positive, is in service to truth.

Every shape life takes is in service to truth because what happens in our daily lives is what brings to light what we are mistaking ourself to be. Only as life takes certain forms do we judge life, mistakenly believe it to be lacking and then desire something different because we feel as if our sense of well-being is dependent on something changing—all of which is an opportunity to see through that misperception into reality.

When a desire is seen through as false and life is accepted as it truly is, it may initially seem as if this is a seeing through of only that particular desire and that it is only acceptance of that particular situation, but it is really so much more when we fully open to it.

If the man with a critical boss had one that was more understanding he would not have the opportunity to see through his desire for approval. After the man suffers for a while within the belief that he needs his boss to approve of him, he begins to question that and then discovers that his true sense of well-being is not held hostage to his boss's opinions.

Seeing through the desire for his boss's approval, however, is so much deeper than that particular desire and situation. He is not just seeing through the belief that he needs approval, he is seeing through the belief in lack—that lack is actually real. He is not simply accepting his boss's words flowing through freely—he is accepting or noticing wholeness now. He senses his true nature, which is a sense of well-being that is uncaused or not dependent on anything at all.

He is not seeing through one attachment or desire that he, as a personal self, has—he is seeing through his belief that he is a someone who is lacking. Seeing through the belief in lack now is actually the seeing through of the very foundation on which the separate sense of self is imagined. Although the significance of seeing through the belief in lack does not initially register this way, as he settles into the 'space of no lack' this truth becomes very clear. Gradually, the openness of this space of no lack registers in such a way that he realizes there is not and there never was anything missing or wrong. He sees clearly that there is not and there never was a separate, personal self.

The discovery that his sense of self is not dependent on his boss's approval, however, does not mean that he may not speak to his boss or even leave his job. But regardless of whether he stays or leaves he realizes that his boss's words have no bearing on who he knows himself—and his boss—to truly be.

Life now is always the opening. Not life in an abstract, mystical sense but life now however it is showing up either internally or externally. Daily life is the mirror clearly, lovingly pointing to wholeness through any projection of a false sense of self where lack and fear feel very real. Grace itself is literally taking shape as the form of the critical words and as the shape of the belief and emotion projected by how those words are interpreted and then felt. There are no mistakes.

When all of life is deeply, unwaveringly understood to be on our side then we are in full cooperation with the evolutionary impulse of Life.

And finally, the third main pointer is that it is the conscious, direct experience of life now that is the discovery of who we truly are.

When we don't consciously experience life now directly, the true sense of who we are remains obscured. And when we do consciously experience life directly, the true sense of who we are is revealed. For those who have not yet consciously glimpsed their true nature, the willingness to now be open to life directly, unfiltered by belief, opens space, so to speak, for truth to reveal itself.

All experience includes what is known and that which knows and the fluid aspect of consciousness in the waking state allows us, consciousness, to misperceive it all—we have that freedom. When we misperceive what is known to be either personal or separate then that which knows is also misperceived because they are really one and the same.

There is no actual separation between form or what is known, which includes thoughts and feelings, and the formless or that which know. So when one is misperceived so is the other, and when one is directly, consciously sensed or experienced so is the other.

It is truly amazing how clear this all becomes when we simply observe and contemplate the nature of experience within our everyday life. Not contemplation of concepts we read in a book unrelated to our experience and not contemplation of what we believe others are experiencing, but contemplation of the nature of actual experience—our own experience. This contemplation does not require any analysis or figuring out. It is pure observation and contemplation of the nature of experience, which is contemplation of the nature of the flow of consciousness in the waking state. And thankfully, the flow of misperception has a very different sense or fragrance to it than direct perception does. If this were not the case, we would be completely lost without any fully consistent inner compass.

Inquiry: Contemplation of the Nature of Experience

When we, Consciousness, believe all the thoughts that come about other people or events then the mind or self seems personal which then creates the impression that life and others are separate, all of which creates a very dissatisfying sense about life and self. We have misperceived 'what is known internally', thoughts and feelings, to be personal which simultaneously and consistently creates the impression that 'the knower' is personal and that 'what is known externally' is separate.

When thoughts are taken personally then we, Universal Consciousness, instantaneously mistake ourself for a very limited personal mind and body and then with complete consistency feel that unnatural constriction as dissatisfying or limiting. But when thoughts and feelings consciously pass freely there is no personal feel about anything, which instantaneously and consistently allows who we actually are to be sensed. Our sense of self appears very different when we are unconscious of self than it does when we are conscious of self.

The significance of this subtle open sense of presence that comes into focus when thoughts and feelings are consciously allowed to pass freely may not initially register as profound or as universal rather than personal, but see for yourself what unfolds as you continue to sense it now. As you continue to welcome the open sense of presence, the distinction between the filtered experience, which creates a false separate sense of self, and the direct experience, which allows the true sensing of self, will become very clear—for those who earnestly remain more interested in peace than in negativity.

The human experience is the flow or dance of Life as one indivisible whole, form and formless. But when we mistake ourself as only form then the dance becomes dissatisfying and fear-ridden. We feel out of sync with the music and the dance doesn't feel natural. And when we discover the reality of our being there is a gradual relaxation into the music, a natural ease begins to flow and the dance is then finally enjoyed. There is a natural synchronicity as form and formless consciously move as one.

The stable realization of truth, however, is never forced on us. The nature of experience within the waking state allows choice. We have freedom to experience whatever we now choose—our judgments or reality, what we believe about life or life as it actually is, who we believe ourself to be or who we actually are, our conditioned sense of self or the natural sense of self. We are free to remain out of sync and to stumble along in dissatisfaction and fear, and we are free to be free of that all—now, in this moment, regardless of what form it is taking.

Some months after the realization, I was brushing my teeth, stressed and desiring to get done as quickly as possible because I wanted to get in bed to read *The Power of Now* by Eckhart Tolle. All I wanted was to be done with what I was doing so I could finally read about being present. When I realized what was happening I stopped all movement and laughed out loud. And in that moment I sensed the wholeness of presence already.

How ridiculous this hide and seek game becomes when we realize that it is only the seeking, the ignoring of what already is, that is creating the impression of hiding. It was only when I believed that life now is lacking that the true sense of life was obscured. 'Get done with this quickly in order to finally be more present' is really the same desire as 'Find someone to love in order to experience love' or 'I need to accomplish this before I can be at peace'. When thoughts are believed the actual, direct experience of life is then filtered. And when life now is filtered through beliefs we just cannot sense that presence, love, peace and wholeness are already now fully and completely what is.

This is the freedom we have at each moment—even at the moment of brushing the teeth. The discovery is truly as simple and immediate as that, which can be verified within your own experience whenever you choose.

There doesn't ever need to be a mystical experience to realize our true nature—just the openness to experience life as it actually is now. And after the realization, there doesn't ever need to be a mystical experience to more deeply sense and express our true nature. It is now or never. It is within this moment of life or not at all.

Allow and Sense: Earnest Effortlessness

Although the pointing within both sections of this book takes the form of a lot of words, it can all be summed up in the following:

> Allow and sense—
> which is another way to say:
> "Be—consciously."

Allow the thoughts and feelings as they actually are and allow how life is now moving as it actually is—and within that welcoming openness sense and express what is.

And although this 'allowing and sensing' at the deepest level requires no effort there is an initial earnestness that is required, which may at a more surface level be considered as effort. The pull of conditioning is to resist and analyze rather than allow and sense and this pull may continue to be quite intense for a while, even for those who have a profound realization.

Earnestness is not needed to be who we already are but it is needed to fully see through who we are not, at both the levels of beliefs and feelings. And to see through who we are not—it is allowing not resisting that opens the way to sensing. Peace is not only the end it is the means because they are really one and the same.

The Paradox of the Search After Realization

Although after the conscious glimpse of truth it may seem paradoxical to simultaneously acknowledge that the discovery is not yet complete, at the same time there is the realization of wholeness now—this is the truth at both levels of experience. At the relative level, we are honest that our current level of experience is not yet a full discovery of reality at the same time that we are experientially aware that wholeness is reality and nothing more than what already is now is needed. Without judgment or grasping for more, our sincere openness paves the way to a deeper realization of truth.

Although, after the realization, there is no desire for more than what is now, there may still be an earnest desire or longing to more fully sense and express what already is. Our acceptance or allowing of what is now does not exclude a longing to more fully integrate or express what is now. The desire to more fully realize what is now comes from true understanding and love, and the desire for more than what is now comes from the untrue foundation of lack, the false sense of a personal self. Those who long to more fully realize what is now are open to however life now shows up, and those who long for more than what is now ignore life now. Love leads the way for those who directly know wholeness, and suffering points the way out for those who continue to believe there is something missing.

All seeking and questioning ceases naturally, honestly—not out of effort or prematurely because we read that seeking is what obscures finding. Regardless of how 'unawakened' it all may seem, it is foundational that we are absolutely honest about our current level of experience. It is not in conscious service to truth to try to convince ourself that what we read or what a teacher says is our actual experience just because the words resonate. There is nothing unawakened about being honest about our current level of experience. It is honesty that paves the way to deeper discovery.

Although there is often the tendency to believe that something is wrong and more is needed when all desire and fear are not blasted out of our system by some mystical experience or that all is not smooth sailing after the realization, this is not the case. When we believe that something more is needed because of rough seas that come, we then ignore life now in search of a future experience that will calm those seas once and for all. We are then completely oblivious to the reality that whatever is showing up right now, even continued conditioned patterns, *is* the actual, literal opening into a deeper sense and stable realization of our true nature.

It is the clear, conscious seeing and experiencing of those conditioned patterns that transmute them into what they actually are, which then allows a deepening sense of what we are. If we pretend that those intense emotional patterns are not there or wish they would go away or accept them as they are believed to be or superficially experience them or dismiss them as an illusion then we are closed to what Life is now offering us. The rough seas are actually exactly what we all ask for—even those humans who are not yet even aware that they are being called Home.

Evolution Is Not Over

More often than not the integration process of the discovery still involves a lot of angst and confusion, but hopefully all of that will gradually change. As more and more humans begin to realize their universality, this process will become more lighthearted and open, and continue to evolve in many other ways.

With more and more of us moving through life with a 'yes', then more and more of those moving through life with a 'no' will more easily sense the unnaturalness of that no. And as humans begin to consciously move from this sense of yes to life now, even without full understanding of that yes, the truth of their being will reveal itself. The honoring of joy, rather than only suffering, will point the way to truth. And then, hopefully, there will come a day when pointing such as this written here will seem a bit silly and the moving through the sense of separation into a recognition of our universal nature will be much more of a natural development, just as moving through the teenage phase into adulthood is. Adults living without a sense of their universality will be in a minority.

Gradually, there will be so much more openness and honesty in sharing how life is moving to deepen our realization, and much more expression that comes from love rather than fear.

Spouses, partners, friends and coworkers will knowingly smile at each other after an argument, and then both will be able to openly and honestly inquire into what is true and share a time of sensing that.

The way we parent our children will also evolve. Parents will nourish and guide their newborns and young children with the clarity of wisdom and love rather than with the confusion of fear or guilt. And as the children mature, parents will parent with the lightheartedness of discovering how life's expression is now moving through their child rather than with a heavy sense of responsibility to mold and influence that expression.

More political leaders will have a deepening sense of oneness with the totality—all humans, animals, the earth and 'the heavens'—and increasingly more decisions will be made from that sense rather than from fear.

This writing is an invitation for each of us to discover our innate sense of oneness and then to move from that. Peace on earth, then, cannot help but to unfold.

Chapter 3

Let It Be

What if all is already fine but because we don't realize that we believe it isn't?

And what if it is only the belief that all is not fine that is the only thing creating the impression that it isn't?

What if, rather than attach to all these various thoughts that come—we just let them be?

How different would our experience here be if we no longer believed what we are programmed to believe?

Imagine no programming. Imagine all in its natural state of complete harmony.

Imagine how different your experience here would be without fear. And then imagine a world without fear.

To paraphrase Paul McCartney who said it so wonderfully in his song, *Let It Be*:

> The answer will come, if we just simply let it be.

This is what is pointed to here—

> Let it be and realize what already is.

Chapter 4

Allow It Fully

Before we realize the truth of who we are we assume that feelings of unworthiness or of 'not enoughness' relate to who we are. And because those feelings, which we assume are the truth of who we are, do not feel harmonious we then try to avoid or change them. We feel we have to change who we are or we try our best to drown out or numb who we are.

But what if those feelings are actually not who you are—but are only covering up who you are?

What if, for just this moment, there is no more avoiding, resisting or trying to change? Why not? Why not just see for yourself what is underneath those feelings?

Without any story, if those raw sensations are experienced fully you can find out what is underneath or prior to them all. Allow them fully, drop through them, so to speak, and discover that which is permanently untouched.

And then, for those who truly want peace, there will be more interest in what is discovered, regardless of how quiet and subtle it may initially seem than in the restless excitement of thoughts.

It is from and as this ever-present space of that which is unconditionally unaffected and unchanging that all is consciously allowed as it actually is.

Realization of Universal Mind: Beyond Time

Nothing is Personal

Chapter 5

Are We Human Having a Spiritual Experience?

Within most, if not all, of the world's religions are two beliefs about truth—that what we truly are is that which does not die and that there is a transcendent or peaceful way of living within this world. The terms used for what we are and for this way of peaceful living are different within the various religions but these two beliefs are largely consistent throughout.

It certainly makes sense that those two beliefs go together because if we truly are not a body/brain organism or that which can be physically harmed, it then follows that we are also not that which can be psychologically harmed—which would then most definitely affect how we live and relate.

But then why do so few actually experience this depth of life that Jesus and others point to since the majority of people on this planet consider themself as spiritual or religious? If we truly are that which cannot be harmed physically or psychologically, why do so many spiritually-minded humans still experience a sense of conflict and fear within and then act out in response to that?

It is partly because we are conditioned to believe that our beliefs are the supreme end all of faith. We believe that it is the actual belief in truth that will create the true experience and then when experience doesn't line up with beliefs we believe that deeper beliefs are then needed. So once again we rely on what is believed, which is really just the conditioned sense of self saying that we really aren't what we believe we are but that we need to become what we believe we are. We believe that there is something now wrong, something is missing, something else is needed so we begin to pray more, meditate longer, study more intensely, go to more gatherings of like-minded humans, and do things in accordance with what we believe even if it means hurting other humans in the process.

None of it ever works very well so we either give up on spirituality and try something else, or we resign ourself to an experience that is a watered-down version of our beliefs. We convince ourself that Jesus and others are only just talking about a heaven when the body dies and don't really mean what they say about a life of unconditional peace and love now—or we become very honest and look deeper.

If belief alone actually produced the experience of what is believed then there would already be many humans living in peace and harmony, internally and externally. 'On earth as it is in heaven' would already be our collective everyday experience since the majority of humans have deep religious beliefs that what we truly are cannot die.

Mere intellectual belief, however, does not create the experience of what is believed. Just as belief in the sweetness of honey does not create the experience of sweetness, belief in unconditional peace and love does not create that experience. Even if we deepen our belief that honey tastes sweet it will not create the experience of sweetness. As long as we hold to the belief that belief will create that experience then it is that very belief that gets in the way of the actual direct experience of sweetness. It is only when, for just a moment, we drop all belief that the possibility finally opens to relax, open our mouth and directly taste what already fully is.

We are not here to believe what Jesus and others taught long ago but to actually discover it. Not in a heaven in the future but now. A peace so unconditional that it surpasses rational understanding, a love so deep that it even includes 'our enemies', a way of life so free of fear that we live without stress and anxiety just as the lilies in the field—all of that is what we are here to realize and express.

The purpose of us being here in this human experience is not to transform who we are but to realize who we are and then live that out. The essence of who we are does not evolve but the integration of the realization and expression of who we already are does. The realization of truth consciously integrates into all levels of our human expression—our understanding, sensing and expressing.

Although we do not become more of who we are through experience, it is within direct experience, not belief, that we become conscious of who we already are. Who we are does not ever need to experience anything in order to be who we already are—but to realize and live that out now we do.

What is it then that we need to experience in order to realize and sense who we are?

Life now. Life as it actually is. All that ever needs to be experienced is Now directly, consciously—not as it is believed to be.

The human dimension is designed for experience and the vehicle in which this human experience happens is the body/brain organism. Although we don't need the human form to be what we are, it is the chosen vehicle for what we are to now consciously discover itself within and express itself through.

This body/brain organism is an amazingly designed vehicle that reflects whatever we are now taking ourself to be. When we don't identify with any thought or feeling, then the human organism reflects an open sense of 'all is well'. And when we take thoughts and feelings personally then the human organism follows suit and also feels personal, and we then feel incomplete. Even the obscuring of truth is in service to truth but that service largely remains unconscious until we discover truth.

In the following quote, the Christian mystic Pierre Teilhard de Chardin points so simply, yet powerfully, through our mistaken identity:

> We are not human beings having a spiritual experience;
> we are spiritual beings having a human experience.

When we mistake our essence as human or mortal rather than Spirit or Consciousness, we have mistaken the human vehicle for our identity. We have believed that we are a limited and separate being which creates a very dissatisfying and fearful experience here on earth. We then feel insecure physically and psychologically, needy and dependent on all kinds of things. Lack and fear seem very real, and control and manipulation warranted, and peaceful living impossible.

Although this one fundamental mistake of identity creates such unnecessary suffering, the good news is that it is just this one fundamental mistake of identity that creates such unnecessary suffering. What stands in the way of the life that Jesus and others speak of is not something that is real or solid or needs to be changed. It is all just an innocent misperception that needs to be seen through fully as false.

The true purpose of spirituality is not to absolve the sinner of sin but to expose the sinner as fiction. We are not here to become a better person but to see through the belief that we are and ever were that which is separate and mortal. And seeing through the mistaken identity of who we believe we are is the very same as seeing through the mistaken beliefs that we have of life now. Seeing through our mistaken identity is the same as seeing through the mistaken belief in lack now—each and every time it rears its head. It is truly as simple and immediate as that.

The belief in lack does not allow peace to be sensed and expressed, and the realization of wholeness now does. Reactions that project from the sense of lack are very different than responses that come from truth.

When stress was experienced while brushing my teeth in the desire of getting in bed to finally be able to read about being present, I believed that life now is lacking and that life would be better when I was in bed reading. If anyone had interrupted me at that time it is likely that I would have reacted impatiently, unlovingly. Because I believed now is lacking and later would be better, their presence would have been interpreted as a delay to getting what I believed I needed. But the moment this internal conflict became conscious it was seen through, and peace and enjoyment in however life is now taking shape revealed itself.

Now is realized as full and complete with nothing lacking. Then if someone had 'interrupted' me there would have been no impatience felt within or agitation expressed without. Now, which includes their presence, would not have been resisted so only openness would have been expressed.

When we discover unconditional peace, this realization cannot help but impact the way we live and relate; but the way we live and relate will not be deeply impacted until we realize unconditional peace—who we truly are.

Chapter 6

Life is on Our Side

Most everyone at one time or another has felt that there has to be more to life than what they are currently experiencing. There is a pull away from dissatisfaction toward lasting peace and fulfillment. With some of us it's a slight tug and with others it's more like a relentless yanking, and so we desperately try to find it and make it lasting through loving relationships, sex, a good job, financial security, more food, less food, different food, health, religion, spirituality, drugs, spiritual experiences, more education, music, activity, being noticed, being left alone—the list is endless. But when peace is not experienced it is always believed that it will be achieved sometime in the future, and what is right now is completely unnoticed.

But what if what we are seeking is hidden in plain sight? What if it is right here, right now and we just don't have the eyes to see, as Jesus said?

The following Islamic saying points so beautifully to this truth:

> I was a hidden treasure,
> and I loved to be known,
> so I created the worlds both
> visible and invisible.

This pull toward fulfillment in the future happens, in part, when we don't realize that daily life is on our side. We believe that whatever is happening now is preventing us from peace and never consider that maybe it is all actually pointing us there.

When our intent is to discover truth or realize peace, why not then be open to the possibility that whatever shows up is in service to that? When there is trust that life is on our side, life now is fulfilling and a completely different dimension of experience opens.

We then see that everything visible is on our side. We realize that everything that happens in our daily life is life moving to wake us up to who we are. The visible is in service to the invisible. The created is in service to that which is uncreated. No matter how it shows up, the world is in service to heaven. It may be heavily disguised or thinly veiled, but what comes and goes is in service to that which is eternally now.

When there is openness to the shape life is taking then life now is our greatest guide. Not a guide in the sense that it will bring us to anything new but in the sense that it points to what already is.

Nonjudgment of this life-guide, however, is foundational. If we resist the form life takes now then we are actually resisting the very hand that is pointing. Peace and freedom are not limited to certain experiences or certain aspects of our daily life. Peace and freedom are the underlying nature of direct experience and are inclusive of the totality without exception. So if this is what we truly want to realize and express then life will facilitate that—the type of person we have been conditioned to dislike and react against will show up, family members will do the exact things that push our programmed buttons and whatever event serves to free us from our conditioned ways of reacting will come. Then all others are free to act as they do and we are free to experience those actions of others consciously, as we actually are, without resistance or judgment but in true understanding and love. Freedom includes the totality or it is not true freedom. Peace includes the totality or it is not true peace.

However life shows up is in service to bringing to the surface whatever beliefs or judgments we still hold—all of which obscure the sensing of our true nature. Judgments believed always create the impression of an incomplete or limited sense of self which is not reality. Life knows exactly what it is doing.

At times, life's pointing may be a deep cutting sword gouging up deeply unconscious beliefs and emotions in order that they are seen and experienced through. If we allow the gouging fully without numbing it in any way with our usual drug of choice, whether it is TV, food, meditation, exercise, music, drugs, reading a spiritual book or whatever our hobby, we may experience some intense feelings. But those feelings are the form life is now taking and when we experience them as they truly are, they point straight as an arrow into the true sense of who we are.

At other times the hand pointing may be a gentle, playful wagging of the finger. Its cooling breeze may be soothing but if we become attached to that seemingly mild-mannered finger and create a positive, personal seeming story around it, it can turn into a dagger on a dime. Life always moves to dissolve the separate sense of self, not to inflate it.

Truth may manifest as a fierce love, which may not be very

comfortable at times, but when truth is more important than comfort then we are open without conditions. When we come to trust the hand pointing in the form of whatever shows up now, we are then in full cooperation with Life itself—we are putty in the Divine's hand.

Chapter 7

Honesty is Foundational

Dishonesty, at any level, delays the realization of truth, and honesty at all levels paves the way. This honesty, however, has nothing to do with telling others what we think of them. It is not about believing our thoughts and then telling others about those beliefs. This level of honesty is about being truthful with ourself about our current level of experience.

Awakening is the deepening realization of universal truth at the experiential level, so if there is any dishonesty about our current level of experience, deeper truth will remain obscured. Honesty about any inner conflict we are now experiencing between the level of our understanding, feelings and actions is foundational. If we deny or pretend on any level because our beliefs don't match up with our feelings or actions, we delay the sensing and realization of truth.

If we have a belief that we are all one or that peace is our natural state but our feelings and actions are out of sync with that understanding, without honesty about that inner disharmony we will not inquire into truth. To dismiss the sense of disharmony as an illusion because we have a belief that it is not real is not in conscious service to truth.

Honesty about what we are now experiencing at the relative level paves the way to the realization of absolute truth. We cannot pretend our way into the experience of peace by learning the language and acting the part—this will only create more suffering and delay what we seek. No matter what the consequences, we have to be willing to be completely honest with ourself. And often honesty begins with coming out of denial that our current level of experience is just fine.

It is amazing how stress, anxiety, restlessness and fear have become so commonplace that many humans don't even sense how unnatural these emotions are. Many, without even realizing it, take personally the endless barrage of fear-based issues broadcast on the daily news. Bedbugs, a new strain of flu, fluke accidents, tainted food as well as so many fear-based opinions projected as fact by some 'newscasters' are all personalized and then felt as significant threats or even as an actual current problem. Life is feared because of what is believed is happening or could happen to them physically or psychologically at any given moment. Yet if asked if they were suffering or dissatisfied with life many would likely respond, "Who me? No, I'm not dissatisfied. Everything is fine—I'm fine." Many believe stress, judgment and fear to be normal and don't even consider that there may be another way to experience life.

But eventually, sooner or later, we all come out of denial. When there is no chore to do, when the TV is off, when the house is empty, when there is no music playing or any book to read there is then the opportunity to become aware of and very honest about the nagging sense of dissatisfaction that has been temporarily ignored and denied. We finally admit to ourself that there is something within us that knows there has to be more to life than what we currently know.

At a deep level we know what truth feels like. This is why we seek it—because we have all experienced it and it feels like home. We may call it peace, joy, happiness, fulfillment, satisfaction, stillness, well-being or freedom but regardless of what we call it all humans, at some level, know this as home.

Some words that could be used to describe the feel of truth are, 'light, free, peaceful, open, harmonious, spacious, joyful, loving, calm, relaxed, without fear, limitless, complete, whole'. No one would use the words 'oppressive, hateful, constricted, conflicted, disharmonious, tense, restless, stressful, anxious, fearful, lacking or fragmented' to describe how truth feels.

But although we have all had glimpses of peace, the price we pay for being within this human experience is the possibility to mistake peace as being caused by some separate object or event. And when we make the mistake of believing that peace is caused by something, dissatisfaction is then inevitable because this is just not the truth. We then chase what we believe will once again cause peace all the while unaware that it is not caused by anything at all.

This is the unconscious human experience—searching earth high and low for the heaven that is already within. But all of that is part of the awakening. Suffering plays a part.

When we come out of denial and become conscious of the nagging sense of dissatisfaction, there is then often a period of time when we believe the answer is found outside of ourself in other people or events. And the flip side of believing the answer is found outside of ourself is that we also believe the problem lies outside of ourself. Desire and fear is the ever-deepening cycle of dissatisfaction. We are forever either trying to grab hold of desirable externals or blaming and fearing them.

Before the glimpse of my true nature, I mistakenly believed objects were the cause of those times I experienced moments of peace. When I fell in love, gave birth to my children, completed a goal or gazed up at the night sky, I attributed the peace I sensed to the objects themselves so for quite some time I thought the answer was in trying to line things up just right.

But then one time, years before the conscious glimpse, there was an experience of profound peace that seemed to have no object attached to it.

I was kneeling on the basement floor folding clothes I took out of the dryer, stressed about getting it done and moving on to the next chore on my list. My mind was swirling and my body tense as I moved to finish quickly. And then my youngest daughter, who was about six years old, came to talk to me. And that time, unlike others, I stopped what I was doing completely and turned to listen to her and it was as if time had literally stopped.

The past and future vanished and there was only complete peace as I looked directly into her eyes. There was no thought as she spoke—only openness. It was an unexplainable peace of great depth sensed in every cell of my body. All mind activity was gone—there was only stillness. It was as if I literally went from one dimension to another.

Within moments, however, it was gone. Thoughts rushed in and peace was no longer sensed. Thoughts of what I believed needed to be done took over and I was back in the stressful swirl of belief.

Although it was a profound experience of peace, I viewed it as a random gift. There seemed to be no sense to it. It seemed completely independent of any object or event and not something that could be consciously chosen. Whenever that experience was recalled over the years ahead, however, it literally brought tears to my eyes and a longing to my heart.

It was not until many years later when I realized that it was not a random gift at all but that it is actually my true nature, uncaused and ever present and sensed only when the 'something is missing or wrong' belief is suspended for just a moment. Because the 'something more is needed' belief was unconsciously suspended the moment I stopped all activity and turned to look at my daughter in complete presence, there was no awareness of choice involved or of its significance. But years later, after the conscious glimpse of my true nature, its significance registered deep and it became very clear that at each moment there is the freedom of choice to sense what is true and ever present or not.

If we can only sense peace when all the chores are done, the sun is shining, the politicians are perfect, the children comply, all the bills are paid, the health is perfect, the house is spotless, our spouse or partner is understanding, our parents are apologetic, or when the planets line up just right then we all might as well either crawl into a hole and never come out, or go to war with life right now and try to whip it into shape.

Those who believe they are victims attempt to control and manipulate life either by withdrawing and resigning themself to a limited sense of self and life, or by fighting to actively change life. The rationalization to 'use violence in order to create peace' is the very same as 'resist life in order to sense life' or 'resist what is now in order to realize the truth of what is now'. Just as we cannot bomb our way into world peace, we cannot resist our way into inner peace.

If anything at all needs to change for us to sense peace now then we are all victims and there is no way out of suffering.

But this is what each of us must discover firsthand—if we really are a victim or not. Even if these words resonate and seem true, please do not believe them. Instead, find out if what they are pointing to is true or not. Put it to the test within your own experience in order to directly discover if you are a victim or not. And if you find that you are not a victim, be open to discover what you actually are.

Whenever you feel that your sense of well-being is held hostage to something notice how that feels inside and then be open to find out in that moment if it is true. Is it true that you are a victim of the weather or a friend's words or the flat tire or whatever is believed to be the cause of the dissatisfaction, or is peace actually now present? And when you are so open that you are not grasping hold of any thought—then notice how that feels inside. You are not creating or imagining anything. You are simply noticing how the conditioned sense of self feels and how the true sense of self feels.

One of the contributions Oprah brought to this planet decades ago and continues to do so on an even deeper level now is raising awareness about our inner state of consciousness. She began by coaxing the collective consciousness out of denial and then out of blaming others into a deeper level of honesty about taking responsibility for our current experience of life, and now in more recent years in pointing to that which is beyond the separate sense of self. Over the years she has consistently pointed to the truth that no one and no event has the real power to sabotage our own power and truth—unless we actually give them that power by believing they do. Within the relative level of experience, the only thing we are ever truly a victim of and a slave to is our own beliefs.

Pointing beyond the belief in victimhood, however, is not to ignore or minimize real physical pain and hardship. In this world people starve, are raped and maimed and tortured. All of that and more happens every day on this planet, and every day some rise above it and some don't. Some who experience great loss find deep peace within while others only become more hardened and sick in their suffering. Some, even in the midst of immense violence, come to know and express peace and love while others only lash out in anger and bitterness either toward themself or others—all of which contributes to the very violence they are reacting against.

Regardless of whether humans overcome some suffering at the relative level or go beyond all psychological suffering at the absolute level, every human being who goes beyond suffering knows they are not a victim. There is not one who goes beyond suffering and blames anything or anyone. It is impossible to go beyond anything without taking complete responsibility for our internal state.

Regardless of whether the sense of victimhood is 'My parents should accept me for who I am' or 'We'd all be so much better off if those politicians would just get along', it is the false belief that our sense of well-being is dependent on something external that keeps us stuck at the level of victimhood.

Sometimes the sense of victimhood stays intact until there is a certain level of forgiveness toward those we believe have hurt us. For those trapped in resentment or blame, forgiveness paves the way out. Blame blinds us and forgiveness begins to bring all into a clearer focus. When we forgive we are open and when we blame we are not, and what comes from openness is very different than what comes from a closed state.

Forgiveness, which requires humility, paves the way for more subtle inconsistencies or dishonesty to come to the surface and be seen through. When there is a certain amount of openness we begin to feel how dishonest it is for us to believe others need to be more peaceful or conscious when we are not. At a certain point, the inconsistency between our own beliefs and actions, regardless of how subtle, becomes unbearable and we are not at all tempted to judge others' actions.

Questions like, 'How can I know peace when others are so unconscious and there is so much conflict in the world?' no longer feel honest. We see that an honest question comes from our own experience. What about me? Is my own experience beyond all conflict and unconsciousness? If not, we are then no longer even tempted to point the finger outward.

When clarity deepens beyond blaming others and we sense that nothing external needs to change in order for us to sense peace now, there is another aspect to this discovery that can open—the discovery that even we don't need to change.

Chapter 8

Are You Whole Already?

Even when we intuitively know that inner peace cannot be dependent on externals changing, many still believe that they need to change. They believe that they are flawed or incomplete in some way and need to be healed or transformed.

But is this really true? Without looking to thought, the truth of your being can be discovered firsthand now.

When you remain open and present and ask the question, 'Is peace now here?', what is sensed? What is sensed when for just a moment nothing is believed and there is only openness itself sensing life directly?

When you listen to the wind blowing through the trees or look at a leaf falling and there is a sense of peace—has anything at all changed? Has who you are been fixed or transformed in any way in order for peace to be sensed?

Could it be that the only thing that is obscuring the sense of peace, the sense of your true nature, is only the beliefs that you now hold?

Could it be that who you truly are is whole already and that the sense of wholeness is only obscured when that reality is filtered by the belief of who you think you are, or of what you think about life now?

What is sensed when life is not filtered in anyway? What is that really? What are you actually sensing when there is only openness to what truly is right now?

Honesty and courage is needed not only to ask the question—but to fully receive the answer.

Chapter 9

Courage is a Necessity

It takes courage to ask 'What is true?' or 'Who am I really?' or 'Is peace now present?' or any other version of that question which resonates, and then remain open to sense the answer because when we sense truth we realize that our beliefs are not there and are not true.

When we sense that well-being is complete and full right now this is the discovery that nothing in life and nothing about ourself needs to change. In that moment we realize that although nothing has changed, peace and wholeness are here fully.

When we contemplate this and remain open to sensing the reality of wholeness there is the possibility for a radical shift of identity.

We discover not only that wholeness is already the reality but that the only thing that obscures the sense of it is the belief that it is not here now, and that it will be caused by some external object or internal healing.

The discovery that nothing external needs to change is a seeing through of the belief in victimhood, and the discovery that we don't need to change opens the possibility for a profound shift of identity. When both are deeply known, we gradually realize that they are one and the same discovery, and the feelings of external and internal dissolve. Life and Self are sensed as one.

Coming out of the belief in victimhood, however, takes courage. Although the corresponding emotions that come from that belief create a miserable experience, at least we believe we know who we are and what our place in this world is. There is a certain comfort in what is familiar regardless of how unsatisfying it is.

Looking clearly, with honesty and courage, at the perceived payoffs of staying with that belief is very helpful in paving the way out.

When we believe that peace will only be experienced if certain things change externally, we then experience either a personal sense of powerlessness or an inflated sense of personal power.

If there is a sense of powerlessness, we get to wallow in our misery, feel righteous and justified in our misery, tell others all about our misery and try to pull them into helping us out of our misery when all the while, we, at a very deep, unconscious level, enjoy it which does not allow us to really receive any of their help anyway.

If there is an inflated sense of power that accompanies the sense of victimhood, then we feel powerful in our fight against life that we believe needs to be changed. Whatever doesn't quite line up with our idea about what should be is a target in that fight. Our spouse or partner, the politicians, our children, the unkempt yard, the wealthy, our boss, our parents, the educational system, our body—no one and nothing is off limits to what we may go to war against next. There is arrogance and a sense of entitlement that life should be as we think it should and there is a deep, unconscious enjoyment in the fight with life. We get to feel right and powerful and make others and life wrong.

All of this is not to say that when truth is realized we just lie back and do nothing. Action may come but it comes from a very different level of consciousness, so to speak, than action from a sense of lack and will, therefore, have a very different impact on the whole since it is consciously coming from the whole.

It takes courage to become aware of the enjoyment that we get from remaining in the feeling of victimhood. Regardless of whether it takes the shape of a powerless or powerful personal sense of self, it allows us to complain and feel justified in those complaints. It gives us a personal sense of self and something to believe in and to do. There is an unnatural sense of aliveness around judging and complaining and trying to change however life shows up.

The perceived payoffs of sticking with the feeling of victimhood can be discovered firsthand by observing for even just a few hours how it feels whenever you judge however life shows up. Even if you don't verbalize complaints, observe how it feels internally to judge whatever is experienced. Feel how satisfying those judgments are at a certain level and how they create an inflated sense of self—even for the one who believes they are powerless. Even in powerlessness there is a false sense of power that can be uncovered. Conflict, even if it creates an inferior sense of self, gives us a sense of personal power and peace does not. Peace has no personal sense of power; we know the true source of power is not personal.

Coming out of an 'I am flawed/I need to be fixed' belief also takes courage and honesty. And here too, it is very helpful to become aware of the perceived payoffs.

When we believe and feel that we are flawed and need to be

fixed this gives us an identity—a personal sense of self and something to do. There is an unnatural sense of restless aliveness around problem solving or trying to find the missing key that will finally cause everything to fall into place. It keeps us seeking and striving, and there is a certain enjoyment in the search and attempt to problem solve. Becoming aware of the enjoyment of this pull paves the way out.

Seeing the perceived payoffs of the belief in victimhood as well as the belief that 'I need to change' is often a process rather than a one-time seeing. Each time these beliefs are exposed for what they are—innocent thoughts believed in—there is an increased awareness of these previously unconscious patterns. And with each seeing there is the possibility of a deepening sense of what is true—as long as all unconsciousness that comes to light is not mistaken for who you are.

Although the conditioning that comes to light may not be very pretty to look at, what you are looking at is only what obscures the unconditioned sense of self—not your true self. Who you truly are is untouched and whole. When this is realized there is no problem exposing what you are not. There is a deeper and deeper willingness to look at it all head on.

Honesty and courage are not qualities that need to be acquired or developed—they are aspects or qualities of our true nature. Truth and the resolve to stand in and as truth, no matter what, are fully already here to be discovered and expressed now in willing openness.

Chapter 10

Even Thoughts Want to be Free

Thoughts are really not a problem. Thoughts alone do not create the misperception of lack or wrongness about life now—but beliefs certainly do.

Thoughts are like free floating energy just passing through consciousness, and they come and go without any problem unless we identify with them.

When thoughts come and are allowed to be as they truly are there is no sense that something is wrong. But when we grasp hold of thoughts it is as if they, and the emotions they create, become frozen in time or unreality and are then dragged along forever coloring truth. A flawed personal, limited self in need of something which will be found in time then seems very real.

Observing thoughts and contemplating how different unattached thoughts feel from thoughts we identify with is very helpful in seeing how that conditioned sense of self is created.

When we observe how different our sense of self feels when we don't grasp hold of any thought, we become more aware of how identification with thoughts instantaneously, and with absolute consistency, creates a limited or dissatisfying impression of life and self. And when we become aware that that unnatural sense of life and self is solely being created by whatever we happen to now believe, the possibility deepens for us to become more interested to look at our identification with thoughts. Naturally, effortlessly we begin to investigate whether that thought-created sense of life and self is actually true or not.

If the thought 'The government is after me' popped into our head not many humans would believe it. Even if there have been past experiences which we could then interpret as proof of the thought's veracity, such as a strange new buzzing on the phone or a blue car that we keep seeing, most of us would not personalize those past events and link them to the thought. The thought would then remain impersonal and pass freely through awareness without creating emotions or causing any changes in behavior. Attention would not fixate on that thought because it is not believed to be personal. That thought would be perceived as the impersonal energy that it is, so the sense that something is lacking or wrong in the form of a personal self in danger would not be created.

But imagine if we were very young and the thought 'There is something wrong with me' popped into our head for the first time. Many of us would believe it completely. Because of past feelings that we have had and interpreted in a personal way, those interpretations seem to verify the truth of that thought. So when the thought is experienced we then link it to those personal interpretations of past feelings. Attention, then, would hook right into that thought, and corresponding emotions and then actions are created. That thought would not only be perceived but it would be interpreted as true. The sense of a personal self that is defective is created in that moment and then dragged along in time to color all experience—until seen through fully.

Whenever thought is experienced as personal information rather than as a perception of energy passing through consciousness, what actually is is then being resisted. Thought taken personally is not allowed, so to speak, to remain in its natural state which then creates a very unnatural sense about reality. But when the thought 'You are worthless' is allowed to remain as it truly is we perceive it purely, which allows the totality to be sensed as it actually is. The thought 'You are worthless' then moves freely through the mind with no belief in it. There is only perception of it moving through just as there is perception of the birds flying overhead. 'You are worthless' has the same feel as 'The government is after me'. Not believed, both thoughts are a bit silly just as if a young child innocently says, "The sky has holes in it!" as he mistakes the clouds for holes. When we directly know there is nothing missing or wrong then people or our thoughts telling us there is just don't register that way.

And even if someone does find that the government has actually targeted them to spy on—from the true perspective there is only clarity and love and any response comes from that. Clarity and love move very differently than fear and hate. The thought 'The government is spying on me' is not interpreted personally, which is to say that from the true perspective it does not have any effect on who they know themself—and the politicians—to truly be.

Thoughts, any thoughts, interpreted personally, even those we believe we can prove at the relative level of experience, do not allow the relative level to be experienced as it actually is—as one with what is 'beyond' it. This relative level of experience then seems personal, which is a misperception with some very dissatisfying consequences. It is a misperception because when we personalize our thoughts we are not just sticking with the bare bone facts of perception at the relative level—we are interpreting those perceptions based on past conditioning. Desire and fear are tainting what actually is. The relative taken personally does not allow the Absolute to be realized, but the relative or temporary form allowed as it actually is does.

Taking thoughts personally creates an untrue adversarial seeming relationship with others and life. But the bare bone facts of life's challenges at the relative level—the car is totaled, the bank account is empty, the body is in pain, the partner left—can be allowed fully without any confusion or effect on our true sense of Self.

Thankfully, we are not our car, our bank account, our body or a personal, psychological entity that is lacking because if we were then life without fear, a life of peace and love, would not be possible.

Chapter 11

Feelings Also Want to be Free: Washing Dishes

A few months after the realization of wholeness and an earnest focus of being present or allowing and sensing life directly, I was washing dishes and there was a sense of complete peace. The water was flowing, soap bubbling up, my body completely relaxed and my mind at rest as no thought that came was believed—all passed through without a problem.

But when my then-husband walked through the kitchen into the basement, strong negative emotions came up and took hold, thoughts popped up with lightning speed and attention immediately hooked into them. Thoughts of 'What is he doing, he shouldn't be doing that. He should be doing this instead' turned into thoughts of an argument that we had a year ago about things that I believed needed to be done, and after several minutes of following this train of thought, I became aware that my hand was furiously scrubbing a pot, my heart was pounding and my face was flushed.

I stopped all movement and literally shook my head as if to wake myself up. As attention went to my breathing there was a relaxation back into life now, my heart slowed down and my body softened. My husband soon came up from the basement and I turned to smile at him. Little did he know how different his return from the basement would have been if he had come up a moment earlier.

I knew Life had handed me a gift and I wanted to fully honor it so I looked at all of that very closely. I saw directly that when attention is not fixated on any thought , only peace is sensed, and that when attention is on what is believed, peace is no longer sensed. It actually felt as if I had been in two dimensions and the contrast between them was immense.

But when I looked more closely at what my attention initially went to, I saw that it wasn't thoughts or beliefs but intense emotion. In this experience, thoughts came after the emotion not the other way around. As my husband passed through the kitchen it wasn't as if thoughts came, were believed and then emotions were created based on those beliefs but rather it was intense emotions that came up which were then interpreted to have a certain personal meaning. When the emotions were experienced I believed the interpretative thoughts that came—that what my husband is now doing is wrong.

But even though I saw all of that and did not believe that how these intense emotional patterns were interpreted was true, that seeing did not prevent them from coming up again and again, pulling attention to them and creating a sense of conflict within and sometimes without.

So over the next few months, Life thankfully continued to allow the conditions for these negative emotional patterns to come up—my husband and others did not do things as I believed they should. So over and over and over again attention fixated on those intense emotions, which went into a story that was believed, and I continued to feel, say and do things unconsciously.

Then one day after getting caught up in this negative emotional pattern, I was journaling about what it specifically was that I mistakenly felt my sense of well-being is dependent on and a memory from the past came to me.

My father was an extremely quiet man who did not communicate love openly and used his words sparingly. The only bit of advice that I remember he gave me was: "Don't procrastinate. Whatever you can do today, get done today." Those words and the way he modeled 'responsibility' through working hard around the house during his free time were taken deeply to heart.

Through the years, this advice became an underlying unconscious life philosophy that linked up with how I was interpreting certain experiences. Over time, as I lived that advice and felt a sense of peace when things were accomplished I then interpreted his advice as true. I didn't realize the sense of peace and well-being as the sense of my true nature when all is accepted and nothing more is desired—I thought it was caused by what I accomplished. So the conditioned sense of self solidified largely around what I specifically believed caused that sense of well-being.

The past was literally living on in the present all the while obscuring what actually is. There was a deep unconscious feeling that the form life is taking now—others doing what they are doing—was not good enough and should be different. I felt that my sense of well-being was dependent on what others, and I, are doing.

The resistance against the simplicity that the form life is now taking—'he is walking through the kitchen'—was held together by an unconscious life philosophy formed in the past and dragged into the present obscuring the true sense of wholeness now.

After I became aware of this previously unconscious philosophy hidden within the emotions that continued to come up, there was a slight softening of those solid seeming emotions and beliefs around responsibility. The intensity and frequency diminished slightly but not significantly. Often, whenever those emotional patterns came up there was still deep forgetfulness and unconscious reactions, which resulted in some confusion and even despair.

The confusion did not have to do with a belief that the emotions had anything to do with what I knew myself to be, but about why they were continuing so intensely for so long. It was all quite confusing because I knew that what is true is not only true at the level of understanding but it is also true at the level of sensing—and expressing.

Although what I directly knew to be true certainly seemed true, I also knew that if it is indeed true it would transfer into all aspects of life. So during the times of disconnect or negativity I did not fall back on what I understood to be true. I remained interested in *sensing* what is true—now, in this moment. My inquiry into truth did not stop when negativity left—it dissolved in the direct sensing of truth now.

And gradually, as I continued to observe and contemplate the nature of experience, always from the position of wholeness which I knew to be true, a deeper threefold understanding eventually took hold.

I realized that this bound energy is coming up to be set free, that it is the direct experience of this energy as it actually is which allows it to be in its natural, free state and also that regardless of how often this same energy pattern comes up, it is now that it is to be consciously experienced.

I observed that just as thoughts that I identify with seem to turn into solid beliefs which then create the impression of a solid, flawed self—so it is with feelings. When I interpreted feelings as personally true it was as if they turned into solid emotions, which then created the impression of a solid, flawed, personal self.

Energy bound either as beliefs or emotions is then dragged along, creating the impression of time and a personal, flawed self with a history. So now when this stuck time bound energy comes up it is coming up in order to be set free, to finally be experienced as the impersonal energy that it actually is. These feelings want to now be experienced directly, consciously, without any identification.

If we believe there is something wrong with these feelings, however, then we have personalized them. And whenever feelings are identified with they are not experienced directly, as they actually are.

A telltale sign of personalization is any attempt to control. If we identify with feelings we will try to resist or alter them in some way by ignoring or indulging them or by pushing them away. When feelings are allowed to be as they actually are there is no attempt to ignore, alter, grab hold of, resist, analyze or numb them. There is no attempt to distract ourself from them by reading a spiritual book, listening to music, or watching TV, and there is no fascination with them. In whatever intensity they come they are simply, purely allowed and fully experienced in the welcoming space of openness.

As the intense feelings continued to come up and to now finally be experienced fully, directly without any identification, I then observed how uncomfortable that is. For decades, whenever those feelings came up the full experiencing of them was deflected by beliefs. Beliefs take the edge off the full direct experience. They keep attention focused on the untrue story of a sense of self that is lacking, but without belief there is no flawed sense of self, and the intense energy of those bodily sensations then has nothing to attach to and nothing to react against because there is nothing that is grabbing hold of them or pushing them away. There is nothing resisting form—which finally allows the full, direct experience of form as it actually is. There is only openness itself allowing all sensations to come and go freely. The energy is now finally absolutely free in the open experiencing of what truly is.

And even though that same pattern of energy came again and again, I gradually realized that it is the fresh experience of life now where the power is. I discovered that life is eternally now, alive and fresh, and that which is only now cannot be sensed through yesterday's stale offerings.

Life is our ally and will take the shape of whatever is in service to deeper discovery. If there are unconscious beliefs or a hidden life philosophy then life will take the shape of the conditions needed to bring that to the surface. No analysis or effort is needed, just openness to life now.

And if there are patterns of bound emotions then life will bring that to the surface as often as is needed for all feelings to now come and go naturally without any personal sense to them.

We remain as the welcoming space for all that comes and goes and trust that nothing more is ever needed than exactly what is now. There is never anything truly lacking.

Chapter 12

The Gift of the Groundhog's Death

After the 'washing the dishes' opportunity when I first discovered that feelings are not a problem, I earnestly remained open to directly experience whatever feelings showed up within my normal everyday life—whenever I remembered, that is. And then, some months later, it was as if life 'upped the ante' and lovingly handed me an opportunity to deepen or widen this understanding by showing up as something a bit out of my ordinary daily life. Life showed up in the form of an accidental killing of a groundhog.

While driving, I was alert when I saw the groundhog a distance ahead come out near the road so I slowed down and watched him as he turned around and began to walk into the field. But just as I was coming up alongside him, a car came up on my left, and he turned back toward the road and quickly darted directly under my car.

Feelings came up immediately and in full force but I resisted nothing. I allowed the intense sadness completely. My body shook, tears came, my heart raced and I was the open space for it all. As all feelings that arose in the body were accepted, I also became aware of how quickly thoughts came up and how desperately they wanted to be taken seriously. Thoughts such as 'If only… Why did you… Why didn't you… What if…' seemed to scream for my attention but I did not engage any of them. Without belief in any thought, attention remained on the full experiencing of all bodily sensations. And then, within several minutes, the raw energy of those feelings was gone. It left completely without a trace. It was as if nothing had even happened. I was amazed to find that there was only such a vast peace and openness.

I knew Life had handed me a wonderful opportunity and I didn't want to waste it so I looked at all of that closely. As I considered how completely the feelings left without a trace, I knew that would not have been the case if I had believed even just one thought that came. In the past when I have accidentally killed other animals, I went over and over the event in my mind, felt sick to my stomach for hours, talked about it with others and felt as if I had done something wrong. My experience felt very personal then because I believed how the conditioned sense of self was interpreting those feelings.

And as I considered the thoughts that came, it was quite shocking to see how insistent they were to be taken seriously. It was as if they were desperately trying to attach to something. Not knowing what was going on and not even attempting to know or to give any context whatsoever to those feelings in my body was unacceptable.

Those thoughts were like a young child stamping its feet demanding to know what was going on and by giving any context or meaning to the feelings through any attempt at all to understand, rationalize, justify or blame that demand would have been met—and the flawed sense of self created. If I had believed one thought the false sense of lack would have instantaneously been created. But with full allowing of those thoughts without identification they faded, no sense of lack was created and attention remained free to directly experience all feelings as they actually are.

Chapter 13

Thought Often Has an Important Function in Awakening

Thankfully, thought is not our enemy. It can actually be a very useful instrument. But thought is only a useful instrument when we no longer identify with it and when we actually use it.

Although thought can never reveal or figure out what is true, it can be a very useful tool in uncovering what is untrue and in deepening clarity between what is untrue and what is experientially known to be true. But if we personalize thought, which is to say that we believe it can reveal the truth of who we are or of what actually is right now, then thought is not in conscious service of truth.

When we identify with thought, we interpret and analyze experience in light of beliefs. When it is assumed that our beliefs and the emotions that follow are true it then makes sense within that misperception to analyze experience based on what is believed. Beliefs, however, are of the past and always take form on the untrue foundation of lack or uncertainty so everything that stems from belief is also untrue. What is directly known does not require belief.

But inquiry into the nature of experience is not what analyzing experience based on beliefs is. Inquiry, before the initial conscious glimpse of reality, is the openness to drop what is believed about now and directly discover life now. After discovery, inquiry, or the investigation of the actual nature of what is discovered, makes use of memory to see through what is false back into the direct sensing of life. When analyzing experience, however, we are a slave to memories forever either trying to understand them or forget them but not interested in the direct, ever-present experience of life which is independent of memory.

After the conscious glimpse, the foundation of all inquiry or contemplation is solidly rooted in what is directly known to be unchanging, and it is from that space that all is seen through fully. Inquiry, when not stopped prematurely, takes us, so to speak, to Stillness—to the true sense of who we are.

When we begin to clearly see, in our own experience, how beliefs and their corresponding emotions create a very different experience than when life is directly experienced unfiltered by beliefs, we become interested in looking at the actual nature of experience. We begin to see that we have a choice to question that 'voice in the head' and in questioning the conditioned sense of self we are questioning the existence of a flawed, separate self and are open to sense what truly is.

But we need to actually take the time to contemplate the nature of experience now, not how we want our experience to be or how we are interpreting others' experiences. At some point even inquiry falls away spontaneously and effortlessly; but initially, until clarity and stability take hold, this contemplative inquiry is very useful and powerful.

Inquiry, however, is not boring or tedious—when it comes from the heart. It is alive, fresh, feels natural and gradually reveals itself as love. Love itself is consciously inquiring into its nature.

If we try to stop stories from running or attempt to manipulate any experience or look at experience superficially or dishonestly we miss the wonderful opportunity life is now handing us. Each moment life hands us a gift in the form of whatever is now showing up. If we give this gift a cursory glance and a dutiful thanks and then go on our way, we ignore exactly what we ask for. But when both hands are open and extended to receive what life is now offering us, regardless of how challenging it may seem, we are then open no matter what.

Before the realization of wholeness, I had a deep desire to be understood, and for some time after the realization this continued to surface. Although at one level I knew that I am really not a victim of what others think of me and that my sense of well-being is not dependent on being understood, when I was completely honest I had to admit that at the experiential level it sometimes certainly felt as if it was. It felt very personal when I perceived others misunderstood me and it felt extremely uncomfortable when I even just briefly considered not trying to fix those misperceptions. To do nothing to fix what I perceived to be a misunderstanding felt intolerable, so again and again I acted on those emotions which led me to try and fix others' perceived misperceptions.

But each time there was forgetfulness I saw what an opportunity it is so I inquired into what is true. This inquiry was not a superficial, cursory type of consideration such as 'I know they are all untrue stories or beliefs and emotions so I can just drop them'. It was an honest, heartfelt contemplation seeing all the way through the false into the true sense of life now. Because this pattern of unconsciousness kept coming up I sensed it would be helpful to look at what I specifically believed I needed for a sense of well-being. So as I wrote in my journal whatever question that arose in the moment, I was, with my whole being, open to sense what is true. My inquiry did not stop until I sensed what is true.

Is it true that I need others to understand me? Is my sense of well-being dependent on what others believe about me? Are my perceptions about what they think of me even true? Can I ever know if they are true? Even if they tell me what they think of me does it really matter? Are others free to believe what they want about me, or do I need to fix what they believe? Can I fully allow them to believe what they want about me, even if they have misunderstood something, and also allow how uncomfortable that feels right now not to attempt to fix it? Is my true sense of self dependent on anything that can ever happen? When is complete peace sensed? What is it exactly that makes the difference between experiencing a sense of peace and experiencing negativity? If there is no change in what I am then what is that difference? And what is it really that remains throughout it all?

Thought is a powerful tool in answering all of those questions except the last one. The answers to all those questions, except the last, help to either uncover what I am not or to discriminate between what is believed about life and what is experientially known directly. The answer to the last question comes as a sense or realization, a non-conceptual understanding, when all beliefs are suspended or seen through.

And although thought cannot go there, it can be an extremely useful tool that brings us to the edge.

Chapter 14

Two of the Greatest Obstacles to Awakening

Sometime after the glimpse of reality, I was putting on mascara and there was a subtle sense of stillness that arose. My hand stopped for a moment and the sense of stillness remained subtle yet distinctly different from what is felt when attention is on thought. It wasn't a profound mystical experience of oneness or bliss—it was an unassuming quiet sense of stillness and peace.

But the conditioned sense of self quickly came back with: "You're making all of that up. You're just imagining that there is something significant about that little bit of stillness." But by that time much of the game was over—I knew. I knew that my conditioned sense of self can't be trusted and at a deep level I knew that whatever this stillness is it is real and that it can be trusted completely.

One of the greatest obstacles to the discovery and stable realization of who we are is ignoring or minimizing this sense of stillness, and another is holding out for an experience with bells and whistles. This is a very strong tendency of our conditioning. Holding out is what we've been programmed to do. The feeling that now is not good enough and then will be better runs deep even with seekers who have consciously glimpsed truth.

We are conditioned to believe that what is ordinary is not enough. The conditioned sense of self wants excitement, something special and extraordinary, something to write home about, something to impress others with—and a subtle sense of stillness just doesn't quite do it.

So when we believe that the subtle sense of stillness is lacking, we dismiss it in order to hold out for some profound mystical experience that we think will transform everything instantaneously. We believe we will fully realize who we are, all will be realized as one, we will be completely free of old patterns and be plunged into an altered state of bliss, and that this realization will express itself fully and perfectly through the human form—all in one instant.

What unnecessary suffering comes with that misperception. Seekers looking, striving, struggling for decades and completely missing what is right now. They wait for something other than what is now rather than remain true or open to what is now. They wait for the bells and whistles of a mystical experience and ignore the natural stillness of life now.

Even if, somewhere in the back of your mind, there is a thought that you will one day have a mystical experience that will change everything in a flash—do not wait. Just let that thought be but—do not wait. Without belief, you will remain open to what is now, in this moment, and then see for yourself what unfolds.

Full awakening is very rarely instantaneous. More often it is a process. First, there is a conscious glimpse of truth, and then a quiet, unassuming increasing sense of what truly is gradually deepens into a stable, unconditional realization regardless of any feelings that may pass through and then, when there is willingness to express what is now, the realization integrates into and through our entire being and into the whole of life.

'Full' awakening, however, does not imply finished by any means. The Catholic priest, Richard Rohr, describes this beautifully in the following quote,

> I love to define mystery as not that which is unknowable but that which is endlessly knowable.

Even when the conditioned sense of self, as well as the patterns of conditioning, has dissolved there is an ever-deepening unfolding that continues to reveal itself.

The glimpse and the subtle sense of stillness, however, if unacknowledged will be obscured. And the quiet, unassuming subtle sense of what is often does remain unacknowledged because it is quiet and unassuming. The realization of the truth of our being is not an 'adding to' with an extraordinary experience but rather a 'subtracting from' of all false notions into a very ordinary, natural way of being, as the spiritual teacher Adyashanti has said.

Stillness, our true nature, is not flashy and is often sensed as a still, small 'voice' which most humans ignore or minimize—and life allows that completely. Stillness doesn't force itself. It only begins to be sensed more deeply when acknowledged.

The welcome mat to both the true and the untrue is attention. Whatever attention is on is fueled. When attention stays on mental chatter then that is fueled and when attention rests on stillness, then what is true is 'fueled' or more fully sensed or revealed. This is because this is what we, Consciousness, have chosen in that moment—what is true or what is untrue. Life allows fully whatever we now choose, in this moment. This is why it is such a significant decision if, after the conscious glimpse, we allow attention to remain on mental chatter *whenever we are aware of it there.* This is a *conscious* choice of the false. It should then not be very surprising when confusion and suffering continue for the one who has glimpsed truth yet remains enamored by the false.

And for those who choose truth and consciously allow attention to rest on stillness, it may seem for a time that the conditioned sense of self turns up the heat and pulls out all the stops to try and hook attention back in. But for those who remain steady in the face of this onslaught, deeper stability will take hold. This 'turning up the heat' is all in service to truth—there is nothing wrong. For the stability of freedom to take hold we, Consciousness, must remain firm in our true stand regardless of *any* thoughts or feelings that come, and this onslaught of conditioned thought patterns coming up to now be experienced as they truly are provides a lot of opportunity for that. The roots of Being go deep, so to speak, when we remain firm in our true stand no matter what comes or goes.

For a time, the conditioned sense of self may even bring up very old wounds that were seemingly long forgotten. Thoughts such as 'What about when you were twelve and you stole from your mother and she couldn't pay the light bill? You can't afford to just stop believing these things aren't important to think about!' may come up from out of nowhere. Or some imagined future scenario may start running through the mind that 'needs' to be thought about right now such as 'What if my daughter doesn't make the basketball team? She will feel so incompetent after yet another disappointment and may decide to carry out her threat of quitting school! My God, she's going to be a drop-out and end up on welfare just like her Aunt Sylvia!'

The conditioned sense of self loves to dramatize and create the impression of problems. The thought 'The sky is such a deep blue today' can quickly go into 'His eyes took on such an intense blue when he told me that he never loved me. He is such a sleaze. Why do I keep falling for such losers? Talk about losers—what about that new woman at work…'

Attention can stay on all of that fiction and we can continue to be 'entertained' by all of our various beliefs, as well as to be blown about and to suffer, or attention can consciously shift from it all and remain rooted in what truly is right now, which has nothing to do with anything conceptual.

Stillness can be sensed right now when there is no longer the need to be entertained by any belief—even the belief that keeps hope alive that one day there will be a profound awakening experience.

Hope, the belief that the best is yet to come and that now is somehow lacking, does not allow the discovery of what already fully is now.

Chapter 15

Allow Attention to Rest on Actual Experience: Presence

Just as hope does not allow the welcoming or sensing of what already is now—so also with all the mental chatter.

Initially, before the realization is stabilized and there is no more forgetfulness regardless of any thoughts and feelings that pass through, there is often a sensing of peace that leads the way to stable remembrance. But in order to sense peace space between thoughts is needed and often, for many, there is initially not a lot of space between thoughts.

Even for those who have had a profound realization, the momentum of conditioning may not allow much space between thoughts. So for those of us with a 'monkey mind on steroids', as was the case with me, there is an extremely powerful pointer to open space, so to speak, which allows what actually is to be sensed—regardless of whether there has already been a conscious glimpse or not.

The pointer from the spiritual teacher Eckhart Tolle, in *The Power of Now,* to allow attention to rest on sense perceptions when engaged in menial tasks was extremely helpful to me initially. This pointer resonated deeply because it can be practiced within ordinary daily life and it quickly proved to be extremely powerful when actually experienced.

Previously, when I did chores attention was on all of my various thoughts—many of which had to do with judging whatever I was doing, wanting it to be done so I could move on to the next thing. This moment was experienced as a means to an end. I was using this moment in the hope of getting to a better one, which of course never came. Because my attention was largely on the outcome of whatever I was doing, this moment or life now was ignored.

But immediately and consistently, when I allowed attention to fully rest on sense perceptions rather than thoughts I noticed the sensing of peace. The vacuum in my hand, the movement and noise of the machine, the crumbs on the floor—initially, there was such amazement in how light and enjoyable it all is. For decades, so many of the chores I had done were just trudged through and now I found such peace and enjoyment in the doing. With no concern for the outcome, I no longer experienced life as a means to an end but as full and complete now.

Earnestly, then, with singleness of purpose, from the moment I woke up to the moment I went to sleep, whenever I remembered, I allowed attention to rest on the hearing, seeing, smelling, touching, tasting, moving whenever I was engaged in tasks that required no thought—which surprisingly involved more of the day than I had realized.

When my eyes open in the morning there is the listening to the birds and to the neighbor's dog barking, the feel of the pulling back of the covers and of the sore muscle as it stretches, the hearing of the cereal hitting the bowl and of my cat vomiting up a hairball, the seeing of the sunlight filtering through the curtains and of the unwashed dishes in the sink—and the perceiving of all thoughts and feelings passing freely. Without any labeling of good or bad, all form is consciously allowed. It is all a very different way of living.

Gradually, I began to notice that within the resting of attention on pure perception there is a still sense of Presence that is not only within but is independent of all that is perceived. Each moment of daily life, when engaged in menial tasks, was then seen as an opening to sense my true nature. I saw housework, yard work, shopping, dressing, eating, cooking, drinking, walking, showering, driving, waiting in line not as impediments to peace but as wonderful opportunities to directly, consciously sense Life now.

Although this direct sensing of life now may initially be viewed as a practice, there is nothing tedious about it. When we open ourself to sensing life now, it gradually reveals itself as a loving meditation. It is Love itself sensing and expressing itself now—in the opening of the mail, the pouring of the olive oil into the pan and in the driving of the car. As any thought or feeling that comes is also purely heard or felt, not only is our true essence sensed but all that is perceived reveals its true essence as one with our own.

For quite a while, however, whenever I talked, listened to or was even just in the silent company of others the sense of truth was obscured by attention solely on thoughts. But gradually there was no judgment of even that as I saw firsthand how all of it is in service to truth. As I continued to contemplate the nature of experience, discrimination between what is experientially known and what is believed deepened and the periods of forget-fulness naturally, effortlessly dissolved. The direct sensing of life now is profoundly Self-confirming—thoughts naturally, effortlessly loosen, slow down and decrease, and the sense of peace and remembrance deepens and stabilizes.

The conditioned sense of self may attempt to project how boring and inefficient it will be not to use every second 'wisely' to think about important things but why not discover directly if that is the truth? Why not see for yourself what is true rather than continuing to blindly believe and act on what you have been programmed to believe?

Initially, allowing attention to rest on sense perceptions may feel as if there is a personal self making an effort to shift and hold attention or to alter experience but these misunderstandings, as well as all others, will gradually clear up as all is welcomed as it is—as shown in the following pointing of the spiritual teacher, Rupert Spira.

> If for many hours our hand is held in a clenched position, the unclenching of our fist will seem, at first, to require an effort. In fact, it is the *clenching* of the fist that requires an effort. However, after several hours of clenching our fist we will no longer be aware that we are making an effort to do so; the clenched fist will seem to be the natural condition of our hand. For this reason the *unclenching* of our fist will seem, at first, to require a new effort. In fact, it is not a new effort; it is simply the *relaxation* of a previously undetected effort.

If we, Consciousness, bind attention in an unnatural, localized exclusive position in the form of beliefs and then relax attention into open, direct sensing—this relaxing may initially feel as if there is effort being made and that there is a separate individual making that effort, but those misunderstandings will clear up.

The real effort is in the binding of attention to thoughts and feelings, not in the allowing of attention and all that is passing through consciousness to be in its natural, free state. The binding of attention is an altering of reality, so to speak—a manipulation of what is.

When attention, an aspect of the flow of consciousness, is no longer bound to the exclusive view of belief, which is some form of 'this moment is not good enough', there is a gradual deepening sense of our true universal presence. All sense of a personal, separate entity allowing what is gradually dissolves naturally.

The true fragrance of life comes into focus when we are no longer attempting to alter the natural flow of life.

Chapter 16

A Walk in the Park

Although life or self is always as it truly is, our sense of life may be very different than the reality of life. We are either experiencing life directly as it actually is or as we believe it to be. We are either sensing our true nature or what we believe ourself to be. And what we happen to believe about life or self is what we have been conditioned to believe. When we experience life as we believe it to be we are really only experiencing the past—not life now.

How the present is perceived filtered through the conditioned sense of self is not the present. How we, others and the world are perceived filtered through beliefs is not the truth. Those perceptions are all a story about the present—not the direct experience of the present.

The compulsive beat of conditioning in some way, shape or form says that 'something needs to be different, something is wrong, something more is needed' so when lack is believed, this programming runs unchecked. Those past ways of interpreting life then continually play out filtering life now. What took form in the past as belief is dragged into the present forever obscuring the true sense of life.

At the deepest level the filters don't alter our true nature at all—it remains as it is just as the sun obscured by clouds remains unaltered. The sun and its warmth is as it is even when completely obscured by dense, thick clouds but the sense or experience of its warmth and presence is most certainly altered—for all that appears as other than the sun.

The moment we take ourself for something separate from source is the moment that the sense of our true presence is obscured. So although filters or beliefs don't truly alter reality, they certainly create the impression that they do when they are misperceived to be who we are. When we misperceive ourself to be separate and lacking then, thankfully, we feel that misperception as dissatisfying. And since we are here to consciously sense and realize what we are, clear seeing of the conditioning or filters that are obscuring our true sense of being is initially very helpful.

Although beliefs always color life now, the specific color reality takes on is based on our own particular slant of conditioning. For those who are conditioned to believe that they are superior then life is colored very differently from those conditioned to believe that they are inferior.

Most everyone, in some way, comes to feel that they don't fit in here, which is actually the truth when we take ourself as a someone who needs to fit into a world that seems very separate. But those who interpret this feeling to mean there is something wrong with them then come to feel inferior. They feel like an alien and believe that others must know something that they don't. And those who interpret the feeling that they don't fit in to mean there is something wrong with others then often come to feel superior. They feel that others are the aliens and that they know something others don't. But both the 'I am inferior' and 'I am superior' perspectives equally obscure reality. Both perspectives solidify the false impression of a personal, separate self, and no one will ever feel fully at home here and now when trapped in either perspective.

The woman who walks through a park identified with her conditioned sense of self that she is superior to most people will experience all she perceives through that filter. When she sees a flower garden she thinks, "The people who designed this didn't know what they were doing. These plants need more shade and those need more sun. This section should have been angled more that way and a gazebo right there would be nice." As she walks on she goes through everything she would have done differently if she had designed it. Then she sees a mother pushing her young daughter on a swing and thinks, "Doesn't that mother realize how dangerous that is? That child is too young to be pushed that high. If I had children I would certainly be more cautious."

If another woman walks through that same park, identified with conditioning that she is inferior to most people, she will experience all she perceives through that filter. When she sees the garden she may think, "The person who designed this certainly knew what they were doing. I could never do anything as creative as this." As she walks on she goes through everything she would like to create but doesn't dare try. Then she sees a mother pushing her young daughter on a swing and thinks, "She seems so good with her daughter—much better than I'd ever be if I had children."

Both women didn't experience Life or Self at all. They only experienced what they believed about life. They only experienced their past. And we always know an untrue experience by the sense of lack or wrongness that is projected. What is untrue has a closed, contracted personal feel to it and truth does not.

There is a very different sense to life when we walk through the park without believing any thought that comes. There is a vast sense of openness. All, as it actually is, is welcomed in the open presence we sense ourself to be. As that presence, we are at home within and as the totality.

All is well as it truly is—the walking, seeing, hearing, smelling, touching and any thoughts and feelings that happen to come and go.

Chapter 17

Three Levels of Experience

Although we, consciousness, at the deepest level are always only experiencing now or life, within this human dimension we could say that there are three levels of experience. When in the waking state, we are either dissatisfied with our experience or we are at peace but believe peace to be caused by something, or we are at peace and directly know peace to be uncaused.

There could be three humans standing side by side silently watching the sunrise over the ocean yet each one experiences life very differently. Although they never say a word to each other and an observer may not be aware of their very different experiences, how they now perceive life determines the level of their experience.

The first experiences life unconsciously filtered through belief. She barely notices the sun rising as attention is on the noisy seagulls and on thoughts about what her husband said to her last night. Her body is tense as she stands there inwardly complaining about the seagulls and worrying about what the day will bring.

The second experiences life directly, yet unconsciously. He relaxes into and opens to life—the sounds of the waves and seagulls, the smells and all the sights—and there is no sense of lack or wrongness about life. There is only the sense of peace as all is accepted fully, nothing more is desired. Yet the moment he turns away from the ocean to walk back to his car, his body tenses as attention goes to thoughts about what he believes needs to be done today and he vows to himself to try and make more time to come back to the ocean. Although he has experienced his true nature, it is an unconscious experience as he mistakes the location or the form life takes as the cause of peace.

The third experiences life directly and consciously. As all form is knowingly allowed to be as it is fully—sounds, sights, smells and any thoughts or feelings that come—there is only the true sense of life within and as the totality. As there is movement away from the ocean back to the car, the forms that are experienced change but not the actual underlying experience itself. Peace remains regardless of any surface fluctuations.

Awakening is about experiencing life directly and consciously now. It is about waking up out of experiencing what the conditioned sense of self believes about life into a fully conscious, direct experience of life—the stable recognition of who we actually are.

The unconscious, filtered experience of Life or Self is commonplace. Most humans don't really experience life at all; most experience only a distorted, tainted, fictionalized version of life based on their particular filters. Beliefs, formed in the past, are carried along all the while filtering what actually is. If beliefs change, the obscuring overlay of experience changes but experience is still filtered nonetheless.

Every once in a while, however, we experience relief from all of that. We may fall in love, get a promotion, have a child, win the lottery, have a mystical experience, watch the sunrise or look at the night sky or even, in complete openness, listen to our child speak and for a moment there is the full sense of well-being. Briefly, there is no sense of lack or wrongness about what is. For that moment, there is nothing else that we believe we need. Nothing is desired or feared so for that moment life or self is experienced directly and all is sensed as it actually is.

Yet, that direct sense of wholeness is fleeting when it is not a conscious sensing, which is to say that we, in ignorance, believe it to be caused by something. When we mistake an object, event or anything at all to be the cause then the sense of wholeness fades because that is just not the truth. That which is causeless cannot be realized when mistaken for something that is caused and therefore can come and go.

Reality never forces itself so if we mistake it for something it is not then it remains hidden. If all belief is unconsciously suspended and peace is sensed and we then believe an external object or event is the source of peace then that will be our experience—a cycle of attempting to find fulfillment in what is believed to be external.

But when belief is consciously or knowingly suspended and the natural sense of well-being is consciously sensed then gradually, if not immediately, our true nature is known as uncaused and ever present.

At each moment, we have the freedom to experience life either as it truly is or as we believe it to be. Although this freedom of choice may not be very apparent before the first conscious glimpse of truth, what is referred to here is the very immediate freedom that is ours to now either judge life or allow life—in this very moment regardless of the shape it is now taking.

Life fully allows both the direct and filtered experience of life—we choose. But when we choose beliefs over what actually is we have forfeited our true freedom for a very limited kind of freedom to now only experience our own particular beliefs, as well as the emotions and actions projected by them.

Chapter 18

Belief Does Not Allow Real Choice

Our universal nature is only sensed when we, consciousness, are not attached to anything. When we identify with any thought or feeling we are being exclusive, so to speak. We have narrowed down our identity from the whole of life to one form.

When one thought is bound the whole universe appears to be bound. When all thoughts and feelings are in their natural state, the totality in its natural state is sensed. This is the power and freedom that is ours which can be directly observed at each moment. Life feels very different when we attach to even just the thought 'When will it ever stop raining?' than it does when that thought passes freely.

The moment we identify with a certain perspective we are beholden to that, and all sense of true freedom is hidden. It then seems as if we are robots to that particular perspective. Although this is not the reality of who we are, it certainly appears and feels as if it is when we choose belief over reality. We then act in ways that we don't want to and don't act in ways that we do want to regardless of how it affects others. This is a hellish level of experience especially for the one who is not denying it and is no longer blaming others for it, yet sees no way out of it.

Living from the conditioned sense of self is a cycle of suffering and discontent without real freedom. We are not free to think, feel, and respond creatively and with real love. The past is obsessively replaying itself which does not allow life now to be enjoyed.

Being born into this world, however, involves taking on a conditioned view of identity—for a while at least. We are all conditioned from a very young age to believe that we are separate and incomplete, and that if we could only just get something additional then we will somehow become whole.

And although we are all conditioned to take on this same false identity, the particular type of incomplete, separate individual we believe ourself to be varies, as well as what we specifically feel we need to become whole or to sense well-being.

If a female takes on the identity of 'dumb blonde' she may feel that how others relate to her physical appearance gives her a sense of worth. 'The intellectual one' may feel that their sharp intellect largely determines their sense of self; 'the rebel' may feel their sense of well-being is linked to bucking authority figures; 'God's favored one' may feel they need to gain and keep God's favor to feel at peace; 'the rape victim' may feel they need attention, isolation or control; 'the peacekeeper' may feel they need conflicts to solve; 'the criminal' may feel as if they need to stand out from others; 'the comedian' may feel as if their sense of worth is tied to making others laugh, and on and on and on.

When an incomplete or flawed sense of self takes hold in childhood and then we occasionally feel some sense of fulfillment, peace, love or even just some relief, we then fall into the trap of feeling that whatever we believe caused that sense of fulfillment is what we continue to need. And what each of us believes we need drives how we behave regardless of how it affects us or others. Although what 'the responsible one' feels they need may not rock as many boats as what 'the rebel' or 'criminal' feels they need, there is no real difference between them. They are all reacting from their conditioned sense of self. They are all slaves to their past.

How can we ever act otherwise when we thoroughly believe we are this conditioned self who needs a particular thing for a sense of well-being? When we believe we are something we are not how can we act free from that belief? How can anyone move in a different way if what they thoroughly believe and feel themself to be is damaged? Unworthy? Superior to those of other races or religions? Superior to those who live in other countries? An individual separate from others? A person located in time and space separate from life? A human having a spiritual experience rather than Spirit having a human experience?

Conditioning is programming. It is like a downloaded computer program that dictates how the computer runs. Programs are fine for computers but for Spirit it just never feels quite right. And what doesn't feel quite right is expressed in all kinds of strange ways. Just as when we wear a coat that is too tight and the body then moves strangely it is the same for Consciousness. When we limit ourself to a body and a personal seeming mind or consciousness then all kinds of unnatural, strange movements happen.

But just as the caterpillar is for a time necessarily woven tightly within the cocoon—there is something undeniable in our DNA that knows we are meant to fly, not crawl.

Chapter 19

What is Nonresistance?

Nonresistance, or acceptance, is a very powerful pointer to truth that can be easily misunderstood. The pointer is not nonresistance to beliefs or judgments as well as the dissatisfaction or fear that projects from them. Resistance has already taken place when we have identified with thoughts and feelings, so if we accept whatever beliefs and emotions that come without seeing them as they truly are we are misunderstanding what nonresistance is.

Nonresistance is allowing or acceptance of what *actually* is—thoughts and feelings in their natural state which have no personal feel to them. No thought, no feeling that comes or goes is resisted. So-called negative thoughts or feelings are allowed to come, and so-called positive thoughts or feelings are allowed to go. Without the labels of positive or negative, nothing is resisted and there is no personal feel to anything. The thoughts and feelings that come and go have no real effect on our true sense of well-being—whether a positive or negative effect.

When events or the shape life takes now are 'allowed' as they are believed to be rather than as they actually are, this is resistance and most definitely does affect our sense of well-being. If our cat doesn't come in one night and we believe that is awful and feel worried about it, and then we accept the awfulness and the negative emotion about what we believe is happening because we want to be in nonresistance, this is a misunderstanding of true nonresistance. Whenever we believe we know what is good and what is bad, or how life should be then that which is prior to all labels or stories remains hidden. What actually is is only revealed when what is believed to be is dropped.

A litmus test for resistance is that if something feels personal or we think we know how life should be then there is resistance. If any thought or feeling affects our sense of well-being there is resistance somewhere which always shows itself as some type of attempt to control or manipulate experience.

Judgments are manipulations of what actually is now—thoughts passing freely. Beliefs are created when we grasp hold of thoughts or push them away. We do not allow thoughts to just be. And when thoughts are not allowed to pass freely they have an immediate personal feel to them. They instantaneously and consistently create the impression that our sense of well-being is lacking or limited. Even positive judgments limit because the nature of that which seems to be personal is limited.

It is one thing to allow resistance or beliefs while being conscious of that resistance, but it is quite another when we remain unconscious of resistance and then believe that acceptance of that resistance is nonresistance.

A man, who has glimpsed his true nature and wants to be nonresistant, is aware that the negative emotions he has toward his mother are created by the belief that she will most likely never accept responsibility for past wrongs. So because he wants to remain nonresistant to what is he accepts those emotions and beliefs. If asked about this 'nonresistance' he may say something like, "Well, I now accept my mother. I accept that she will most likely never take responsibility for what she did and I accept the emotions that sometimes come with that reality. Some negative emotions still come but I allow them fully."

But when he accepts beliefs and emotions he is accepting them as true, not as they actually are. He doesn't see through the beliefs and emotions to what actually is. He doesn't see through what he believes his sense of well-being is linked to, which is another way to say that he does not see through his conditioned sense of self. Acceptance of judgments and the emotions they create is not true acceptance.

Even the belief that 'my mother will most likely never accept responsibility for what she did' is of the past. There is still the belief that it would be better if she took responsibility and that she should be different than he believes her to be. His sense of well-being is still linked to that limited perspective. Although this story may be a more refined one than 'my mother is an awful person', it is still a story and still obscures the true sense of what actually is.

Although he wants to accept what is, he remains unaware that what truly is is resisted when he believes *any* thought. Any identification with thought is resistance of his true nature. When he believes the thought that he knows that it would be better if his mother accepted responsibility he takes his stand as a person who is dependent on external factors for his sense of well-being. He believes peace and love are caused by something, completely unaware that they are not caused by anything at all.

But if this man were conscious of the identification with the thought that it would be better if his mother was different yet resistant to letting that belief go, *then* it is very helpful for him to consciously allow the resistance to letting that identification go.

He is aware that he is resisting what actually is by grasping hold of the thought that his mother should be different, yet does not want to let it go because of how good it feels to believe that he is right and his mother is wrong. He is then conscious about not wanting to let that belief go and honest about why.

And then after suffering for a while longer in conscious resistance to truth, he becomes willing to let go of the feeling of being right. He now only desires truth. Then, in a moment of pure open acceptance, while he is on the phone with his mother, he hears her talk about the snowstorm that is supposed to come tomorrow and he senses only peace in that open hearing. As thoughts come about what she should talk about instead, he is amazed to discover that there is only peace in the open hearing of those thoughts also. As she continues to talk, he senses that all is well just as it is, and he becomes aware of a deep sense of love which includes even his mother.

Later, as he contemplates all of that, he sees that if he had believed even just one thought that came while he listened to his mother, the true sense of his and his mother's essence would have been obscured. He now sees directly that as all is allowed to be as it actually is, the sensing of peace is here. And in that open sensing, all traces of the personal, even of the solid seeming concepts of 'mother' and 'son', are not there interfering.

Although nonresistance is allowing what is to simply be, this allowing not only involves the 'passivity' of not grasping onto or pushing away thoughts and feelings. It does also have an 'active' component to it.

Nonresistance is a *conscious* allowing *and* sensing of the totality as it truly is. When form, which includes thoughts and feelings, is consciously allowed to be in its natural state then there is the opportunity to consciously sense the source of all form.

And when we consciously allow and sense what actually is, we soon discover that it is not a dead, static experience. It is alive and fresh; and when the totality of reality now is acknowledged, however subtle it may initially seem, there is an opening to depths of life that cannot be imagined.

Chapter 20

Fear at the Level of Thoughts and Feelings

Not all fear is the same. We scare ourself unnecessarily when we believe our thoughts and the sense of reality is obscured; but this fear is different than fear that arises when there is a suspension of beliefs yet not a recognition of reality.

All fear that comes is an opportunity to allow and sense what actually is. Fear created by beliefs is an invitation for the beliefs to be seen through back into the true sense of reality. And fear that arises when beliefs are suspended and there is not yet an experiential knowing or sensing of reality is an invitation to experience this fear without identification back into the true sense of reality.

The man who believes the thought, "It will be awful if I lose my job" scares himself unnecessarily by believing that thought. He mistakenly believes his sense of well-being is tied to what happens externally, so he then suffers.

But after suffering awhile he becomes interested in looking a bit deeper so he begins to consider what he is believing. And when he honestly looks at the belief "It will be awful if I lose my job" he has to admit that he doesn't know. He clearly sees that he just simply does not know if it will be awful if he loses his job.

And for one moment as he opens to not knowing if it will be awful if he loses his job, this not knowing expands to the totality. He becomes aware of an openness that truly knows nothing, and in that moment when all beliefs are suspended intense fear arises.

But he allows the feelings, experiences them completely, and he allows all thoughts that come without believing one. Nothing is resisted. All is allowed as it actually is without any identification; and when those sensations called fear dissolve there is only an open, vast stillness of great depth—and now he knows.

He has seen all the way through belief into the true sense of that which is unknown conceptually yet known experientially. If he had stopped when beliefs were just suspended and fear arose, and he then identified with those sensations, he would have resisted the gift life is offering. If fear comes when beliefs are suspended it is a gift that need only be experienced fully, purely, to open.

If fear is created by beliefs and we don't see that and then allow that fear, that fear will likely be experienced again and again until those beliefs are seen through. Those fears are arising in order for the beliefs that are creating them to be liberated. To allow that fear without clear seeing of the beliefs creating it is not true allowing.

And if fear arises when beliefs are suspended and we resist the full experience of those sensations because we believe any thought, even the thought that there must be belief somewhere because of this fear arising, then those sensations will likely come up again. These fear sensations that arise are an invitation to experience them purely without belief in *any* thought that comes.

One way to tell the difference between fear created by belief and fear that arises spontaneously when all belief is suspended is whether or not we think we know something. With fear created by belief we think we conceptually know how life should be. But when fear arises when belief is suspended there is a glimpse of not knowing anything conceptually, yet not a glimpse into what is experientially known.

When truth is glimpsed fear dissolves because what we truly are is not frightening.

Analysis and effort to figure out whether fear is created from belief or is arising spontaneously when all belief is suspended is not needed.

Life knows exactly what it is doing and makes the way clear for those who are open.

Chapter 21

That Which is Permanent is Also Uncaused

Life is very dissatisfying and frightening when all we know is the impermanent, that which comes and goes. Nothing seems reliable, trustworthy or satisfying, and so we desperately try to grasp hold of what we believe will bring a permanent sense of satisfaction.

The search for happiness or peace is really a search for something that is permanent or ever present unconditionally. Everyone, whether they are conscious of it or not, is trying to find something that doesn't come and go. And regardless of whether we try to find it in relationships, money, success, drugs or spirituality this search can all be boiled down to a search of permanent well-being. We are all searching for our natural state of complete harmony—the truth of who we are.

But what is permanent or ever present is also uncaused. They go together. What is permanent has to be uncaused otherwise it is not permanent. If something is caused or created it can then also leave. It can die. What is created is always beholden to the concept of time. Only what is uncaused or unborn is permanent—timelessly present.

So how can the one who has not yet consciously glimpsed that which is uncreated sense what is uncaused by anything at all? If nothing they do can cause what they already are to come into being, how can they ever sense the truth of who they are? The truth of who they are is sensed the moment they simply stop misperceiving that they are what they are not. When we stop misperceiving what is caused, thoughts and feelings, as what we are then the uncaused comes into focus.

Sometimes, however, those who have a conscious glimpse of truth know it as permanent and sometimes not. With some, the glimpse of their true nature registers in such a profound way that they know it to be unconditionally present even with forgetfulness and continued unconscious reactions, while others believe their true nature to be impermanent when there is forgetfulness. Rather than only the sensing of truth temporarily being obscured, some actually believe truth to be gone.

Those who have glimpsed truth and know it to be permanent, even though there is forgetfulness, have glimpsed beyond the foundational belief of lack but are not yet stable in truth. And those who have glimpsed truth and believe it to be impermanent are still caught up in the foundational belief of lack, which keeps the false sense of a personal self intact.

Those who realize truth as permanent yet still experience forgetfulness see clearly that the impression that something is missing is only that—an impression created by belief. But those who believe truth to be impermanent because there is forgetfulness believe that truth is missing, that lack is actually real.

This is a very significant distinction because if, after the glimpse, there is forgetfulness and it is believed that truth has dissolved then it is also believed that something not only caused it to dissolve but that something caused it to come into being. They believe they did something to create truth and they did something to dissolve it so they will then try to replicate the conditions they believe caused it and avoid the conditions they believe dissolved it.

The misperception that our true nature is not permanent and is caused by something must be cleared up in order for stability to take hold. Those who are still caught up in the belief that forgetfulness means their true nature is gone must find out directly if that is true. They must discover if it is true that stillness, peace, wholeness, awareness or however truth registers for them is not now present, even without the conditions they believe caused it. Even if they have the belief that truth is permanent they must put aside even that belief and directly *discover* if truth is present each moment it is now felt that it is not.

If this misperception is not investigated and cleared up these seekers will be stuck in a cycle of attempts to recreate conditions that they believe are needed in order to create truth. Desire and fear will hound them as they try to manipulate life. Their actions will be locked into attempts to control their thoughts, feelings, and movements trying to get back Home to what is already fully here.

When the truth of our being is experientially known to be permanent unconditionally there is then a rooted foundation on which all conditioned patterns can be experienced through. This firm, unshakeable foundation is essential to the dissolving of these patterns because otherwise they will be mistaken for who we are, and confusion and misperception will continue.

But when we know that which is permanent then even the intensity of those patterns being flushed up in order to finally be set free cannot move us. The most intense emotion can come and we know absolutely it is not who we are. And when those patterns are transmuted and no longer trapped in time, all forgetfulness falls away and the stable remembrance of the timeless unfolds.

Chapter 22

The Truth Sets Us Free—When We Know the Truth

The realization that nothing needs to change changes everything, so to speak. We go from believing that something always needs to be different to realizing that nothing needs to be different. We go from feeling that our sense of well-being is dependent on all kinds of things to realizing that our true sense of self is not dependent on anything. The entire feel of experience changes when we know that nothing needs to change for us to sense peace.

And gradually, the significance of the sense of peace begins to settle in. Trust deepens as we realize the sense of peace as Home as well as that which is leading us Home to the full, stable remembrance of our true nature without any more forgetfulness.

But although the sense of peace leads the way after the first conscious glimpse of reality, before the first glimpse it is often the sense of dissatisfaction that helps lead the way right toward the edge of truth.

Before the first glimpse, if the persistent sense of lack is followed honestly and courageously all the way back to its true source it brings us to the edge of reality. When the sense of lack is traced back through denial and then back through blaming externals, then often what is believed to be our greatest flaw is temporarily mistaken to be the source of the sense of lack.

Regardless of whether we believe our greatest flaw is control issues, anger, gossip, or an addiction to sex, drugs, work, TV, keeping busy, food, accumulating money or possessions, lying, stealing, or any other numerous possibilities, we believe that if we could just get this part of our personality under control then the sense of lack would finally leave and we would find lasting fulfillment. But with fresh eyes and open heart this sense of dissatisfaction believed to be caused by a personality flaw can lead right to the edge of reality.

As a woman obsessively cleans her surroundings, she comes out of denial about the sense of lack and then gradually traces it back through blaming others, to blaming herself, to questioning her beliefs about the source of the sense of lack and then opens to what truly is.

But initially, she denies any sense of lack. She tries to convince herself and others that she is happy and life is fine and that the obsessive cleaning is not a problem even though her children and husband react against it. But then finally, when the conflict within the family becomes so intense, she is driven to go deeper. She becomes more honest with what she is experiencing. She finally admits how unhappy she really is, and how this need to clean does seem to have control of her.

Initially, however, when she first begins to look at what is causing this unhappiness which then causes her to obsessively clean she sees that the obsession becomes strong when she is angry, so she then believes that others are the problem. Depending on what happens she believes her children, husband, boss, mailman, plumber, store clerk, waitress, parents or politicians are to blame. She believes that if others would just be the way she thinks they should be then all will be well, and she wouldn't be driven to obsessively clean. She believes the source of the sense of lack is external.

But then, after she suffers a bit more in the negativity she has toward others, she becomes a bit more honest about what she is experiencing. She comes to see that she doesn't just obsess about cleaning when she is angry at others or life, but also when she buys new shoes, when someone compliments her, when she sees a new cleaner advertised on TV, when the sunlight filters through the curtains a certain way and hits a crack in the wood floor and on and on. She then admits that others are not to blame, but then believes she is to blame. She believes the source of dissatisfaction is an internal flaw, a part of who she is, so she thinks that if she could just fix herself and get this cleaning obsession under control all will be well.

But after some more suffering through failed attempts of therapy, medication and reading numerous books on the subject to try and get her behavior under control, she becomes very honest. For the first time she looks directly and boldly and with absolute honesty at the persistent sense of dissatisfaction.

She sees clearly that even before this cleaning obsession took hold, she was largely dissatisfied, and thought numerous other things would fulfill her and dissolve the sense of lack. She had to admit that what she believed would finally fulfill her kept moving and changing and never really delivered lasting peace and fulfillment.

So rather than blindly continue to try and eliminate that discontent by means that have already proven to be unsuccessful, she begins to wonder about the times when the feeling of lack did leave and she was at peace.

She sees that throughout her life there were brief periods of peace. Fulfillment was experienced but never lasted. She would get what she wanted and feel fulfilled, and then always come to believe that something more is now needed. Without exception she sees that was the pattern, that what she originally thought would fulfill her and seemingly did for a time was now not enough.

And because this peace consistently showed up whenever things lined up the way she wanted, she assumed those things were the source of peace but now she sees that they aren't. If those externals were the source of peace, the peace would have lasted as long as those conditions were there, which she sees was not the case.

But in those brief periods of peace it truly was as if nothing was lacking, so she wonders about the source of peace. If the lining up of externals the way she wanted is not the source of peace, then what is? What else is consistently there during all those experiences of peace?

And in a moment of profound clarity she sees that when peace is experienced there is not only a lining up of externals or desirable conditions, but there is a moment when all is internally accepted. In that moment she accepts life fully. There is no longer a belief that anything is lacking or should be different, and it is in that moment when peace is sensed. She sees that even if those desired external conditions were there and she did not internally accept life, but instead believed something more is needed, she would not have sensed peace.

So then she wonders that if peace is sensed when all is accepted and nothing more is believed to be needed—could it actually be only the belief that more is needed that creates the impression that something is missing? Could it actually be that lack is not even true, that nothing is wrong, that peace is now present?

So she asks with pure sincerity and with no intention other than truth itself, "Is peace now present?" She remains open to sense what actually is now without looking to thoughts for any information.

And she becomes aware of a subtle sense of peace which contains no lack. She allows this peace to just be without any grasping, pushing away or attempts to understand it. As thoughts about what her boss said to her last week come, not believed, they flow through her mind freely and the sense of peace is untouched.

Then her child barges into the room and screams, "Mom, he did it again! Tell him to stop!" and the thought, "Why can't they just get along for one hour?" comes and is believed. Emotions of anger and resentment are then felt and she reacts according to those emotions, and within minutes of dealing angrily with her children and setting them each up with a chore, she begins to vacuum the house even though it clearly does not need it.

Initially, she judges herself and feels that 'this peace thing' is all hopeless and maybe she needs to wait until her children are out on their own before she can experience lasting peace—but then she becomes more honest. And immediately, after she admits that the children are not to blame, she becomes aware that she just can't ignore how much like home the sense of peace is. Even though it was a brief and subtle sense of peace, there is something about it that pulls her interest; so rather than come up with another plan to try and stop herself from obsessively cleaning, as she would have previously done, she is now more interested in peace.

As she contemplates all of this, she sees that when nothing is believed there is no sense of lack, and that the moment she believes her thoughts there is. The thought of what her boss said to her last week wasn't a problem because in that moment she didn't believe it. But she sees that if she had, the sense of peace would have been obscured, just as it was the moment she believed the thought that her children should just get along. Immediately, there was the sense that something is wrong and peace is absent.

So she looks at the belief that her children should get along and wonders if it is true. Is it okay that they argue? When what is actually happening now is that her children are arguing, is it true that they need to be different for her to sense peace? Is her sense of well-being really dependent on anything that happens? If the thought 'Why can't they just get along for one hour' comes but is not believed, is the sense of peace still present?

So she allows the thought 'Why can't they get along' to just be, and remains open to sense life now. And again, she observes that when she allows her thoughts to just be she becomes aware of a subtle sense of peace that she simply cannot deny. And gradually, as she continues to observe her thoughts or see through any she grasps hold of, she becomes aware of the consistency of peace. She realizes that peace is unconditionally present even when the sensing of it is obscured.

Peace feels more and more like home and the feelings of anxiety and worthlessness that still come feel increasingly more alien and more quickly recognizable as false, and gradually she comes to recognize this sensed wholeness as somehow being the truth of who she is. And with this gradual shift of identity away from beliefs to wholeness, there comes an unshakable willingness to look immediately and unflinchingly through identification with thoughts. An intense earnestness takes hold within her.

Her sole purpose then, from the moment her eyes open in the morning until the moment her eyes close at night, is to sense peace and see through any beliefs or emotions that obscure it, rather than to try and control the cleaning obsession. For the first time in years, the cleaning is a nonissue. Truth now, in this moment, is her sole intention.

So as she continues to obsessively clean again and again and judgments of that come, she sees through all of them fresh each time. She sees through all beliefs and experiences through all feelings allowing all thoughts and feelings to flow freely. Gradually, the moments of remembrance increase and lengthen, and she begins to sense the profound power of this open allowing and sensing.

Wholeness is where she steadfastly takes her stand, without one drop of judgment that is left bound.

No matter what—no matter what she does, how much she cleans, how angry she acts toward her children, how confused she may be, what judgmental thoughts come—she plants herself firmly as the open sense of wholeness.

Although she doesn't understand it, she deeply knows there is no lack and she trusts this sense of wholeness completely. She knows it as true and she knows judgment and negativity as false, so it is always from the true foundation of wholeness that she observes and contemplates experience. It is always from the foundation of her true nature that the false is seen all the way through.

When we take an unwavering stand as Wholeness, freedom reveals itself within the entirety of our human experience.

But that stand as truth must be uncompromising.

This is the truth that sets us free—when we know it.

Chapter 23

True Intelligence

Could it be that there is Intelligence beyond conditioned thought—and even beyond clear reasoning?

Could it be that even pure reason can only take us so far, and then trust, letting go, opening to that which is beyond or prior to all reason allows the true understanding?

Universal Mind is universal. It is the field, substance and flow of the totality. How can that which is universal ever be sensed or known by anything other than that which is universal?

Even pure reason is only a temporary, limited appearance in the whole so it can only go so far. No appearance within the universal can ever sense that which is universal.

And when that which is universal mistakes itself for a fragment, it is then impossible to sense its own reality. When we take life now for what it is not, reality remains hidden; and when we do not misperceive life, reality is revealed.

St. Francis of Assisi points so simply and directly to the truth of our being with the words, "What we are looking for is already where we are looking from." When our 'looking' is fresh and free of conditioning then we realize the universality of what is looking, and when the looking is filtered through programming we don't. Universal Consciousness comes into focus when we, Universal Consciousness, perceive Life now directly and consciously.

And when that which is universal is directly known this

knowing includes the totality so not even one speck is left behind. If one thought now appears to be bound, if one feeling now appears to be bound—it comes for that. All is set free and all is in service to the setting free. True Intelligence is pure love which does not exclude or waste anything.

Not even a grain of sand is excluded or wasted. There are no exceptions in what is set free and in what is in service to this setting free.

Life, the formless, form and fragrance, knows exactly what it is doing.

Life is pure, unfiltered Intelligence flowing as whatever shape is now appearing.

It is all alive and it is all calling us Home.

Do you hear the grain of sand calling your name?

It says, "Love."

Do you sense the truth of it?

If not, lean in and 'listen' again—

this time with the whole of your being.

Chapter 24

Allow and Sense: Stories of the Rope and Necklace

Sometimes there is a recognition of who we are not, yet not a clear recognition of who we are. Seeing all the way through what is believed, however, is not only a seeing of what is false but a sensing or recognition of what actually is, as pointed to within the following two stories when contemplated together—the first of which is an adaptation of a pointing from the spiritual teacher, Mooji.

There were two friends, Mary and Sue, who liked to get together occasionally for a weekend visit. One weekend it was Sue's turn to visit Mary's home and when she arrived they greeted warmly, and then Mary pointed upstairs and said, "Make yourself at home. You know where your bedroom is." So Sue went upstairs, opened the bedroom door, took one step inside and screamed. Mary ran up and asked what's wrong, and Sue pointed and said, "A snake!" Her friend entered the room, looked where Sue was pointing and saw immediately what had caused Sue's misperception. There was a sheer cover overhanging a side table and under the table was a rope. From where Sue was standing the sunlight filtered through the cover and made it appear as if the rope was a snake. So Mary said, "Oh, it's just a rope. Come closer and look this way so you can see directly without the filter of the cover." So Sue did and saw clearly that there was nothing to fear—it was just a rope.

That evening they went out for dinner and hours later when they came back Sue went up to her room, turned the light on, took one step inside and screamed. Mary ran in once again and asked her what was wrong and Sue pointed and said, "A snake." Mary again saw clearly what the misperception was. She saw that from where Sue was standing it made the rope appear as if it was something to fear so she invited Sue to come closer and look directly without the filter of the cover. And, immediately, when Sue looked directly she realized that there was nothing wrong—it was just a rope.

They stayed up past midnight that first night together enjoying each other's company and then Sue said she was tired and went up to her room, turned on the light, took a step inside and screamed. Mary ran in and asked what was wrong and Sue pointed and said, "A snake." Mary again saw immediately that it was all just a misperception, that from where Sue was standing it made it appear as if the rope was something it was not, so she again invited Sue to come closer and look directly without the filter.

This forgetfulness went on again and again throughout the weekend, and Mary each time invited her friend to see for herself. Mary didn't tell Sue to just believe her and she didn't tell Sue to rely on her memory, but fresh each time she invited Sue to see for herself directly—which Sue did. And immediately, with unfailing consistency, with each clear seeing Sue's fear dissolved.

And then toward the end of their time together Sue went to her room, turned the light on and stepped in and saw what looked like a snake and some fear came but she didn't turn away this time. She didn't call out in distress. Something made her take a step closer and look directly *through* the filtering cover this time, and her eyes cleared and it was as if the filter wasn't even there as she saw what actually is come into focus. All fear dissolved and she was amazed to see that even the filtering cover is not a problem.

Whenever there is belief in the 'something is wrong' thought and feeling we are taking our stand as a personal, separate someone who believes they need something to be different for their sense of well-being. But when we inquire into truth, by either consciously suspending beliefs or consciously seeing through them, and then stop that inquiry simply because the fear or the wrongness about now dissolves, we have stopped prematurely. We have stopped before our true stand is directly sensed or known. Inquiry is not about getting rid of suffering—it is about discovering or confirming truth now. True inquiry ends or dissolves in Stillness, not just with the understanding of what we are not.

The sage, Ramana Maharshi, when asked by a woman to show her the way to have "the happiness of Self-realization", pointed to Truth in the following story:

> A lady is wearing a necklace around her neck. She forgets it, imagines it to be lost, and impulsively looks for it here, there and everywhere. Not finding it, she asks her friends if they have found it anywhere, until one kind friend points to her neck and tells her to feel the necklace around the neck.

He did not say the kind friend points to her neck and tells her the necklace is there. He said the kind friend points to her neck and tells her to *feel* the necklace around the neck. To only tell her friend the necklace is already there her friend would then have to believe what she is told; but to tell her friend to feel the necklace around her own neck it is pointed out that she now has the opportunity to discover directly what is in her own immediate experience.

Because we are not some separate object we can never discover what we are objectively but, as Ramana is pointing to, there is a very distinct sense to our true essence that when consciously opened to can spark recognition. This distinct sense is even known in deep sleep as an infinite sense of well-being that is only veiled in the waking state when we misperceive what is and then feel as if it is not here.

When the 'snake' or identification with thoughts and feelings dissolves, there is then the opportunity to sense what actually is. But we have to be open to that sensing and to be open we must drop all expectations about how we think it should feel. If the lady with the necklace around her neck has any expectation at all about how the necklace should feel then she is not really open. And without openness she will miss what is literally right under her nose.

What Is may initially seem very, very subtle—but don't underestimate its quietness. See for yourself what unfolds as you acknowledge it, open to it and follow it all the way Home.

Following the sensed essence of truth is what Mooji points to when he says, "When you're quiet you realize you are the way—you're not following a way."

Realization of Universal Body: Beyond Space

Nothing is Separate

Chapter 25

Stillness Moving: Deepening Sense of the Whole

We are here not only to realize the truth of our being but to express it. If we realize who we are but still move from fear or a sense of obligation or cultural expectation, then the realization has not yet integrated into the whole of life.

When there is some level of realization we are then lovingly given the opportunity to move from that realization, which is the very opening to an ever-deepening sensing and expressing of truth. Sometimes this comes as a surprise to those who realize their true nature but when we see through our conditioning it should not be very surprising to then find that conditioned ways of expressing ourself begin to feel alien. We don't realize truth and then continue to move from fear or a sense of need or lack. Life doesn't move that way—consciously.

Before we realize truth we make decisions from the conditioned sense of self which is obsessively judging life now to be lacking. Beliefs about what should be done to work toward some sense of well-being in the future dictate what we do regardless of how we really feel, or how it may interfere with what others want. Past programming is in charge of what we do and how we express ourself now.

If we are conditioned to believe that we should have a certain amount of money in the bank before we retire, that it is better to take a less desirable job that includes health insurance over a more desirable job without health insurance, that we should always weigh a certain amount and make sure we exercise each day, then our actions will be an attempt to uphold those beliefs regardless of stress or how we really feel.

And if we are conditioned to believe that supper should be on the table at a certain hour, that the children need to do their homework right when they get home from school and that they need to go to college, that we should never decline a friend's invitation or certain traditions need to be upheld during birthdays and holidays, then those 'shoulds' and 'shouldn'ts' drive our decisions regardless of stress or how we and others really feel. A fear-based sense of obligation or cultural expectation motivates our actions.

But when conditioning is seen through and that whole foundation for making decisions collapses—how then do we move within this new way of being? If all the 'shoulds' and 'shouldn'ts' are gone, if the sense of well-being is full now and nothing more is needed to secure it—how then are decisions made?

After the realization and a deepening sense of truth, I gradually noticed how differently my body feels when thoughts and feelings pass freely than it does when there is identification with them. When all thoughts and feelings are free, my body is relaxed; there is no sense of stress. And when there is identification, my body is tense and my stomach feels tight.

After a while, this sensitivity to my body very gradually increased to the point that I could often immediately feel whenever there was resistance. And then something happened during a vacation my then-husband and I took in Maine, which was the opening to a deepening sensitivity and commitment to how life is now moving.

We were driving back from visiting friends an hour away from where we were staying, which is quite rural. There aren't any grocery stores near it and as we drove through a large town I remembered that we needed some things at the store and asked my husband to stop at the supermarket coming up. But immediately my stomach tightened and I realized that if I shopped right then I would be rushing through the store, stressed. As I considered whether I should go in or not my thoughts told me that I was being silly and that I should just push through the stress and get what we needed. After all, we were here in town anyway, there were just a few items and it wouldn't take long at all. A little stress never hurt anyone, right? It was all very tempting but my body just did not cooperate with my thoughts and I decided to listen to my body instead. And instantly, in that very moment, there was an all-pervading sense of peace.

As I considered all of that, I realized that the decision to move with how the body feels now is a conscious decision to move with the flow of life rather than in resistance to it and in reaction to what the conditioned sense of self believes about life—even in the 'smallest' of decisions.

From that moment on then, I consciously, earnestly committed to only do what can be done in acceptance or conscious presence—no matter what. This was a decision to never again consciously push through the stress, and I trusted that I could 'listen to my body' to sense how life is now moving.

Whenever I remembered from that moment on, each time there was something it seemed needed to be done, I paused to consider how now doing that felt within the body. If my body tensed I did not do it then. And whatever I did do I only did for as long as I could do it in full acceptance. This meant that sometimes things that I started did not get finished right then. Literally, I might wash a few dishes and then feel my body need to move on. I might even get half the items on my shopping list and feel my body need to move on. My commitment to move freely with what is right now was more important than getting things done.

This was a huge break from my conditioned way of moving and it didn't take me long to become aware of the 'payoffs' of conditioning. This allowing of the body to move with how life is now moving is often not without 'cost', or what appears to the conditioned sense of self as cost. When we do things from a personal sense of self more is likely to get done, others' expectations are more likely to be met, and there is a temporary inflated personal sense of fulfillment.

When we've been conditioned to get things done in order to feel good about ourself and then we realize that nothing needs to be done in order to sense well-being, the doing motivated by a sense of lack falls away. There may then be a period of settling into this natural way of being that may not initially involve a lot of doing before a more natural, harmonious and spontaneous way of moving arises. The holiday cookies may not be baked this year, the decorations may not even be brought out, the house renovations may come to a halt, and the yard work may not get done as quickly or as thoroughly or maybe not at all. And then some or all of that may start up again or some completely new and unexpected movements may begin, but whatever is now done is done in joy rather than to fill some perceived lack. The doing in the hope to gain fulfillment or approval or anything at all is vastly different than the doing for the sheer enjoyment of the doing.

If the holiday cookies are baked, they are baked in joy not because of a sense of obligation. If the yard work is done it is done as an expression of joy, not out of some need. Stress doesn't factor into anything as we move in, from and as joy.

The personal sense of accomplishment dissolves, the concepts of failure or success become meaningless, things begin to shift and people close to us may voice their disappointment or wonder what in the world has come over us. But this also is what is, and when accepted without a story it is not a problem. When others' reactions are allowed as they truly are there is no attempt to ease it, fix it, understand it or judge it, and our sense of self remains unaffected. We realize that who we are is not held hostage to others' opinions. Our true commitment remains solely with truth, no matter what.

Initially, this deepening sense of life's flow may begin as a commitment of 'checking in with the human body' but after some time even that falls away. As the feelings of boundaries dissolve, the body then begins to move more spontaneously from a natural sense of what is. There is then no distinction between flowing with life and flowing as life. We realize there is only life, our true universal body.

The human body, however, is only free and in its natural state when we are not identified with anything. When we identify with thoughts and feelings, the body is the servant of those beliefs and emotions, and cannot be trusted to reflect truth. When believed, thoughts dictate how the body feels and should move. Beliefs create emotions and emotions create unconscious reactions and movements of the body. So the untrue experience at the level of thoughts becomes an untrue experience at the level of the body and then into the world.

Liberation from personalizing thoughts and feelings opens the opportunity for us to now experience the human body without personalization. But it is just that—an opportunity—not a given. There are those who, to a certain level, awaken from the conditioned sense of self but when life then wants to move in ways that are far outside their conditioning, they opt out.

Awakening is movement that most certainly brings about the end of our world as we know it, as the teacher Adyashanti wrote and speaks about. Consciousness, now consciously knowing itself, integrates this understanding into our full human expression by the very willingness to move in response to truth rather than in reaction to fear. And the more fully the realization integrates into our human expression, the more fully we understand, sense and express that which is beyond our human expression. We come to see how this human expression, which is actually consciousness itself, is 'the way in' to that which is 'beyond' it.

This is the integration of the realization into the whole of life—movement in response to and as the unconditioned whole.

And although this movement is never in reaction to fear, sometimes it is made in the midst of fear. Movement in reaction to fear is a conditioned response stemming from identification with the belief that something is now wrong. Movement in response to the whole is unconditioned movement without identification with any thoughts or feelings that come. With unconditioned movement fear may arise but without identification with those sensations there is no attempt to control anything. All thoughts, feelings *and movements* are allowed to be as they actually are. Even in the midst of those sensations called fear, it is directly known that nothing is wrong.

All fear that comes in this process of integration is an opportunity to more fully realize and express our true nature.

How could it be any more perfect—to discover and express that which is infinite and timeless within and through and as what appears as a limited and mortal form?

Chapter 26

Bold Movement in Alignment with Truth

When we don't experience life as it truly is, life feels frightening. It feels separate, we feel vulnerable so we then try to control life. But when life is experienced as it truly is, it ceases to seem frightening. It no longer feels separate, and the sense of vulnerability dissolves along with all fear-based attempts to control life. But to experience life as it truly is at the level of the body does not only mean within the body as feelings but through the body as movement.

Within this human dimension life moves, it flows, it expresses itself. There is a constant flow of energy as form, within form and through form. So when there is some level of understanding about what we are, Consciousness then begins to move consciously. And as we move consciously, we then more deeply sense that our individual expression is actually not separate from all other expressions, as well as from Life itself.

Mystical experiences are not required to blast fear out of our system and for us to stabilize in the sensing of oneness with the totality—only the willingness to move with however life is now flowing. With conscious movement now, all sense of separation between life and self dissolves, and life free of fear is realized and expressed.

Decisions and actions from the conditioned sense of self reinforce the false feeling of a limited, vulnerable self and fear continues. Movement in alignment with how life is now moving gradually dissolves any residual feelings of separateness from life, along with fear.

This movement in alignment with truth is bold because it arises from the unconditioned and moves in unconditioned ways. Conditioned reactions are often predictable, and unconditioned responses are not. With conditioned reactions we believe we know what will happen, and with unconditioned movements we rest in not knowing. Conditioned reactions are motivated by fear and fear-based actions have very limited outcomes; while unconditioned movements are responses from the whole, and when responses are in harmony with life itself, there is no telling what may unfold.

How the conditioned sense of self projects this movement free from past conditioning makes it seem very frightening, so all kinds of arguments against it may come up—even the argument that no movement should be made until all fear dissolves. But if this argument is believed then fear will continue. Fear dissolves in willing movement with the whole.

It is as if there are two dimensions being experienced simultaneously. At the surface there may be a lot going on, even fear, but underneath it all is a steady, ever-present, unshakeable, profound peace. If peace or well-being is believed to be gone then there is identification that needs to be seen through. The sensing of unconditioned movement remains largely obscured until the truth of our being is known directly to be permanent and the sensing of peace is trusted. With this inner integrated understanding and sensing, a deeper sense of life's flow comes into focus. There is a knowing that does not come from rational thinking. There is a sense of how life is now moving and sometimes this movement involves moving even in the midst of fear. With willing movement in the midst of fear there is no attempt to internally control those sensations and no attempt to control how life is now moving. When all feelings and movements are allowed as they actually are, there is a direct knowing that all is well.

Movement in alignment with truth may initially only involve actions within relatively minor areas of daily life. Hours at work may be voluntarily cut back, how free time is used and who it is spent with may gradually change, what we eat, how we eat, even where we eat and numerous other 'minor' actions may shift. But when these willing shifts in movements are in response to the whole, they are significant no matter how small they may seem.

And then at some point in this unfolding, movement in alignment with truth may involve willing shifts within major areas of daily life. We may find that we move out of long-term friendships or intimate relationships, change where or how we live, or leave or change jobs.

All of these willing shifts, however, are in natural, effortless response to the whole of life. They are not forced or planned. We sense how life is now moving and we are the welcoming space for it.

There is the sensing of how life is now taking form and we move with and as that.

There is no resistance, no attempt to manipulate or control life's flow—only a full allowing of it regardless of where it takes us.

Chapter 27

Fear at the Level of Movement

Even when desire or the belief that more is needed is seen through and the sense of lack dissolves, there may still be occasional fear and a feeling of separation in certain areas of life. For some, even though there is a profound sense of invulnerability beyond any psychological identity, there may still sometimes be a feeling of vulnerability at the level of a perceived physical identity. Intense fear around the comfort and safety of the body may still be experienced within certain areas of life. And although this fear may feel very intense at times, there is nothing wrong with it. It is an invitation into a deeper sense of reality.

Certain aspects of life are feared when life is felt not only to be separate from itself but separate from who we are. Life feels as if it is broken into parts, and certain aspects of life we feel safe in and others we don't. This is like feeling that there are only certain aspects of ourself that we feel safe in and others we don't and that it is self that is fragmented.

So when we realize that our sense of well-being is not dependent on anything and there is therefore nothing to fear, life then gives us many opportunities to now 'walk the walk'—even within those specific areas of life we have been conditioned to fear. What is known internally now has opportunities to externally express itself. And in that very movement, life then ceases to seem fragmented within itself and separate from Self, and the seeming validity of fear gradually, naturally, effortlessly falls away as the feelings of internal and external dissolve.

To live without fear we first have to live with it consciously—as it actually is. To move without fear we must now move consciously even in the midst of fear. Movement in the midst of fear, but without identification, dissolves it and reveals the essence of life absent of fear.

Life is whole and flows as the whole—it needs nothing, wants nothing and fears nothing. It is completely without lack and separation so there is never anything that is ever truly needed or feared. But for truth to integrate this level of realization within all aspects of our experience, willingness to express this directly-known reality within the entirety of daily life is foundational.

The specific areas of life we fear are as varied as the conditioning each of us takes on. Some may have fears around employment or possessions while others don't at all. It may be that in the area of finances we trust life completely and do not move from fear in that area, but in the area of health we do. Around issues involving money then, we move without any sense of anxiety or pride or the need to control, but around health issues we move in reaction to fear along with the need to control.

Fear arises in those areas of life that we don't trust. We are conditioned to feel separate from life in those specific areas, and what we feel separate from we don't trust. And when we don't trust life we feel as if we have to control it or help it out in some way.

Identification and control go hand in hand. Whenever we identify with the feeling of fear there is an internal attempt to control those feelings and an external attempt to control life. Without identification with those feelings all attempts to control what is experienced within and without fall away.

So now, without identification, we have the opportunity to finally experience fear consciously, directly, purely. This fear, which is different from fear created by identification with thought, arises spontaneously—so there is no belief to be 'seen through'. As all sensations are allowed fully this then allows the body to move freely. Internally, these sensations are consciously, directly experienced; and externally, there is only movement in alignment with the Whole. All is allowed as it actually is. Without identification, reality is sensed directly. There is no confusion.

Jesus demonstrated this movement perfectly when faced with the unknown of what may happen. In the Garden of Gethsemane when he cried out in agony for this cup to be taken from him, there was fear. But quickly, he surrendered fully and moved willingly into the unknown of each moment as his physical body was tortured and killed. When on the cross and near death his words, "Father forgive them for they know not what they do," point to the depth of that surrender. He moved willingly each step of the way right through his literal crucifixion without any confusion—even about those who killed him. Any fear that may have arisen along the way, such as when he cried out, "Father, why do you forsake me?" was quickly seen through and did not cloud his knowing of reality.

Willing movement in cooperation with how life is now moving is vital to integration. If there is a conscious decision not to move in alignment with truth, the suffering will be greatly intensified, and the fear that is experienced there is different than fear that arises spontaneously without any identification. The intense fear that comes from a conscious decision not to move with truth is an opportunity to see through the beliefs that have been identified with. Love can be fierce at times but it is always only Love.

When fear is experienced it is an invitation to allow and sense life as it actually is—the loving whole rather than as a scary fragment.

In my own particular integration process (thus far) there were many encounters with fear all related to specific areas of daily life. The two major areas of life that I was conditioned to fear and try and control were in the areas related to responsibility and finances—areas that often went hand in hand.

Interestingly, these fears took root during certain experiences with my father or, more accurately, during my identification with how those experiences were interpreted. Because my father's words and actions were interpreted personally, I identified with a self whose sense of well-being is dependent on being responsible and financially frugal and secure. And over time I came to feel that the more responsible I was in all areas of my life—with my money, my time, my husband and children, my body, others, my job—the more fulfilled I would feel. 'Be responsible' was the mantra of the conditioned sense of self, and what was believed to be responsible action was of course all past conditioning. Identification with that programming kept me in a loop of actions motivated by fear.

When my commitment to 'responsibility' shifted to truth

alone, however, Life then gave me many opportunities to now move 'irresponsibly' or freely even in the midst of fear that arose spontaneously, not from belief.

So in spite of what would have previously been viewed as irresponsible, financially and otherwise, there were many decisions or movements that came in response to truth rather than in reaction to conditioning. As mentioned, fear still arose at times, even intensely, but it did not stop me from moving with truth—for long at least.

At some point after the realization of wholeness, I knew the realization was not full so I sent out a heartfelt Yes to whatever is needed. No matter what I was open. Soon after that Yes there were several unusual challenges that came, which were accepted and opened to, and then in the midst of it all there was a profound increased sensitivity to the flow of Life. It literally felt as if I no longer fit in certain places, and it soon became clear that I was to leave my marriage. There was only love and acceptance for my husband yet a knowing that I could no longer be in the marriage. So even though this was far outside my conditioning, which dictated that I be responsible at all costs, I was willing.

With my decision to leave the marriage there was initially only deep peace and clarity that admittedly, at one level, felt a bit strange given the circumstances. But then, a day or two later after reading five words on a computer screen and interpreting them personally, intense fear and confusion came up and I ended up telling my husband that I am willing to separate for now rather than divorce.

Immediately, despair set in. For two days I barely slept and I felt sick to my stomach. The contrast between the sensed peace and clarity just days ago and that despair and utter confusion was immense. Yet in the midst of all of that, there was a moment of clarity when I knew I had to physically leave the home. So within a day or two I moved out and then with raw honesty looked directly at what I had identified with. I began to consider what it was specifically about those five words that scared me.

The words "I wish you well, Mom" that were written at the end of my daughter's e-mail, an e-mail that gave no indication of judgment, were interpreted in a personal and dismissive kind of way. I took those words to mean that she was writing me off although there was nothing she said or wrote to indicate that.

So I considered all of that. I considered whether I was willing to leave the marriage *even if* all three of my children and other family members 'wrote me off'. Was I willing to be so 'irresponsible' to jeopardize my relationship with my children and others? Was I that willing? And after deep, honest contemplation I knew I was.

Clarity returned as well as a profound sense of peace. There was a deep knowing that divorce is in alignment with how life is now moving and, regardless of any fear that may come, I was willing. This unconditional willingness to move with truth, regardless of where it took me, was the very opening into an immense, unfathomable Love. When the decision to divorce was made once again, a vast sense of Love for only That Which Is filled my being—and for this Love there was nowhere I would not go.

I realized that there are no mistakes. There are only openings each step of the way, when our eyes and hearts are open enough to see and receive them. It became clear that the contrast between the intense suffering and confusion experienced when I 'turned my back on truth' and the deep sense of clarity, peace and love, when there was willing movement once again, was instrumental in increasing the steadiness of movement.

So over the next months, as more movement far outside my conditioning was willingly made, even in the midst of some fear, there was an unfolding of stability, a steadiness of movement that was not previously known.

Chapter 28

Love's Embrace

The integration of the realization of who we are cannot only be postponed if we are unwilling to accept life's invitation to move with the unconditioned whole, but also if we don't relax into it when we do accept the invitation.

When we move with how life is now moving there may be a tendency to brace ourself, to bite our nails in anticipation of when life becomes a bit more familiar. There is then the possibility of falling into the attempts of the conditioned sense of self to try and control life. We may try to figure things out or help life along, but when seen clearly even this is an opportunity for a deeper relaxing into the unconditioned.

But there is also another way this process of integration can be postponed. If our intention either in the moving or in the relaxing is in any way personally motivated this is a sure way into confusion and suffering.

If our intention is to get something out of it such as, 'I'll move and relax in the hope that I will at least get some inkling of where this is taking me' or because of fear such as 'I'm afraid of what may happen if I don't move with life or relax now that I have moved', these are sure ways to postpone this unfolding.

The Unconditioned won't be bribed—and it doesn't respond to fear.

Love is its language and it only moves with and as that.

Love meets Love as we allow and embrace life now, without

any intention other than that very 'meeting'.

Chapter 29

The Kingdom of Heaven

Jesus said, "The kingdom of heaven is like a merchant seeking fine pearls, who, when he had found one pearl of great price, went and sold all that he had, and bought it."

"Again, the kingdom of heaven is like a treasure hidden in the field. When a man found it, he hid it again and then in his joy went and sold all he had and bought that field."

Jesus didn't say they sold everything and then went to look for something of great value. He said they found something of great value and then sold everything to buy it. After they discovered something of value they, in their joy, were willing to let go of all they had in order to obtain what they had found.

When we consciously glimpse peace or wholeness and realize it as permanent, at some level, we know its significance. There may not be full understanding of its significance but we know it as ever-present truth. Gradually, when we continue to acknowledge and confirm truth we realize it as our true home—as what we actually are.

And when the significance of that reality settles in to a certain level there is no price too high that we, in our joy, are unwilling to 'pay to fully obtain it'.

The Kingdom of Heaven or the integration of the realization into the whole of Life is not something of the future, however. It is fully within this moment that there is a 'selling' *and* 'buying'. It all unfolds fully now—the dissolving of conditioned ways of moving and the allowing of the unconditioned expression.

Life knows exactly what 'selling and buying' is in service to the 'obtaining' of the Kingdom of Heaven. We don't need to try and figure it out. It reveals itself each moment, and in unconditional openness we sense it and respond with willing movement now.

Two months before the divorce was final, it became very clear that the teaching position I was in was no longer for me so I resigned. There was no rational decision-making process involved in that resignation. It was as if an intense flow of energy was moving my body out of the job and the only choice was to move with truth or stay in opposition to truth and suffer. I chose to leave.

Everything about that resignation was far outside of my conditioning. To resign mid-school year, leave students and staff seemingly in the lurch, go without medical and dental insurance without even knowing what the divorce settlement would be, was something I never would have done previously. Although the conditioned sense of self would have done the 'responsible, safe' thing and toughed it out at least until the end of the school year, there was freedom of movement as no thought that came was believed. There was only peace, clarity and love as I continued to work at the school for the next two months to fulfill my contract requirements.

But although there was an underlying peace with this resignation, at the surface I did notice some fear around losing dental insurance but not medical insurance. For some crazy reason the image of me ending up toothless in a gutter shook me until two days after my resignation when I watched the documentary, *I Am*. When I saw the clip of Gandhi smiling, showing just a few remaining teeth as only pure love radiated from him, tears came to my eyes along with a heartfelt Yes to whatever life has. If I am to end up toothless in the gutter then there is willingness for even that. Little did I know that Life lovingly had more deepening opportunities in store for some more residual fear to be flushed up and moved through.

The divorce was final on the same day of my first day of unemployment and one week later a tooth started to act up and the dentist told me that I needed a root canal. Fears then kicked up in full force.

Fears of not having enough money to take care of myself and of being toothless and destitute on the street once again seemed to possess my body. Even though I had enough to pay for what needed to be done without being left penniless, intense fear arose. And simultaneously with this fear also came an urge to attend a retreat with the spiritual teacher Francis Lucille across the country in California. This urge came from out of the blue and was strong. I had never before had even the slightest desire to be with a spiritual teacher so this urging, which I wouldn't call a desire, was completely unexpected and very intense.

So even though fear continued to arise and even though I previously would have considered it irresponsible to spend money on a retreat when I needed surgery and was without a job, within two days all arrangements were made to attend.

And when all arrangements were set and the thought 'What the hell did I just do?' came, I did not believe it and then, immediately, there was the sensing of lightness and joy and all fear dissolved.

After contemplation of the fear that arose, the willing movement even in the midst of it and then the dissolving of it, I became very aware that life is giving me opportunities to become more comfortable with and spontaneous in this new way of being and moving, particularly in the area of finances. Trust in this area of life, or life as the whole rather than as fragmented parts, was deepening. Not trust in the sense that I believed I would always have enough money to live comfortably, but trust—deep, unshakeable trust—that no matter what happens it is absolutely fine and has no bearing at all on what I am.

So the day after all the arrangements to go to the retreat were made, and the car battery died and I sat at the garage waiting for it to be replaced, there was only peace as I again consciously realized what an opportunity this all is.

And then a week later when the GPS went and then only days after that the computer—all I could do was smile and welcome it all fully. After I was told how much money it would take to fix the computer and there was full acceptance of letting go of that money, an image popped into my head of a translucent female figure standing with arms outstretched freely letting go and freely receiving. There was only a free flowing stream of energy which ran through her, and a deep sense of freedom and love enveloped me.

Although these, as all, accounts of the unfolding can create the impression that it is all some big event that happens over time—that is not the deepest truth of it. Even though at a more surface level it could be viewed as a process that happens over time, at a deeper level it is always 'in the moment' fully. It is a deepening unfolding that is always revealing itself now, regardless of whether it is in the moment of the handing in of the resignation letter or in the walking down the hall.

The sensing that resignation from my job is in alignment with life and the moving with that is not any more significant than now listening to my student speak or in eating a carrot. Freely expressing life now, in the listening and eating or however it now moves, *is* the unfolding. Each movement is either a conscious expression of the Whole or not. The step walking down the hall can be a step taken in suffering or truth.

There are no moments that are more significant than others. There are no big or small expressions of life—there is only Life. However life is now moving is the invitation into and as that flow consciously.

The Kingdom of Heaven is eternally now. So when the electric bill comes in the mail or when we are making supper while the children are running around and there is a noticing of some tension—*this* is the moment of 'selling and buying', of letting go of conditioning, and of sensing and expressing the Unconditioned. Conditioned ways of opening and paying the bills or of making supper while the children are running around feel very different than unconditioned movements of opening and paying the bills and of making supper while the children are running around.

The Kingdom of Heaven is sensed and expressed now, within this very moment, or not at all.

Chapter 30

Can I Be Awake and Still Dye My Hair?

For quite a while after the realization, I had some very solid beliefs about how an awake being would live, as well as how truth would feel. Gradually, these beliefs loosened and the image widened, but that widened image still had boundaries. There were still notions that all awakened beings would hold the same political views, eat the same foods, spend free time in the same way, not dye their hair and on and on—and also that it *must* somehow feel different than the very ordinary seeming yet profound sense of peace and love that is my experience.

So when the urge came to be in the physical presence of a teacher there was also the sense that I wanted it to be in an informal setting. I wanted to more fully experience the teacher's expression other than when he was just teaching. So when I saw that Francis Lucille, a teacher who I resonated deeply with, would soon be holding a weeklong retreat in his home, attending that felt right.

And during our first lunch together when I sat down next to Francis and he expressed some radically different political views than my own, after getting over the initial shock, I realized how perfect this all is. If he had been more guarded and not as free there would not have been the opportunity to be shocked out of those fixed notions I still had about how truth would express itself. I realized that what is free is free, and that what is truly free does not have a fixed look about it. It has a consistent, loving sense but not a fixed look.

There was also another encounter with Francis that week which was an opening into a deeper understanding of this free expression of love. As we stood next to each other around a table of snacks, munching and talking, I blabbered on about something and Francis' neutral yet clear response was an absolute gift. When I finished talking (about something which I later realized was clearly motivated by a personal sense of self—fear) Francis turned and looked at me directly in the eyes for several seconds with an open, neutral expression, then slowly turned his head away and without saying a word walked away. The initial felt impact of that response was quite neutral yet later revealed itself as love.

Over the months following this retreat with Francis, there was not only an unexpected emptying out and opening up of my own views, political and otherwise, but a gradual relaxation into both the ordinary sense of peace and love and the 'imperfect' expression of this love within and through my human form. Notions of extraordinary bliss as well as limited views of what true expression would look like faded.

When life wants to express itself as what most would view as kind and compassionate no one objects. But when life wants to express itself as what could be interpreted as insensitive or rude, how many would still be willing? If life wants to consciously express itself as it sometimes did through Jesus when he called others hypocrites, fools, serpents, blind guides and a brood of vipers, would we be open to that expression of love—either in the receiving of it or in the speaking of it?

And I realized that just as we can be attached to making sure we always come across as kind, we can also be attached to being a vegetarian or vegan, not dying our hair, not using makeup or wearing jewelry, making sure we use our free time only for 'spiritual' activities or to numerous other concepts. When we lock ourself into a certain way of being with all of our preconceptions, we close ourself off from life now.

It is so much more enjoyable to let go of all notions about how we think we should live and just move with what feels most joyful or authentic now regardless of how *anyone* may view it—our parents, children, partner and even our beloved teachers.

Chapter 31

Life Without Fear Also Includes the Fear of Imperfection

Some of us are conditioned with a fierce streak of perfectionism to the degree that even after the stable realization of who we are, there is a feeling that any conditioned reactions at all are unacceptable. We feel that only unconditioned movements should now happen.

But what if regardless of how profound the realization and integration of that realization is, occasional 'blips' or conditioned movements still happen? Not patterns of conditioning and not conditioning that creates a conditioned sense of self—these are something of a different matter altogether—but occasional loose ripples of conditioning. We may sometimes find ourself saying or doing something that we see is from conditioning rather than from that pure place, but instead of denying, dismissing or fearing this 'imperfect' aspect of the human experience, why not see it clearly and fully relax into it?

Without any concern of image and with full trust that those conditioned movements are in service to truth, even for those others who may interpret those actions personally and suffer because of that, then the totality is opened to fully without fear. When we identify with any concept at all, even the concepts of 'perfect' and 'imperfect', we delay the relaxing into that which is prior to all concepts.

Any fear around 'imperfection' is a censoring of life now, and when we censor life we simply cannot sense our innate, natural joy.

Chapter 32

Owning Without Owning

As long as we believe and feel that we own anything fear will hound us. The fear of others or life taking it from us is kept in place within the belief of ownership. Our sense of well-being is then bound to what we believe is personally ours and affected whenever we believe what is ours is threatened or not enough.

Regardless of whether that fear manifests at the individual level as anxiety or internal conflict, or at the collective level as war or external conflict, there is no real difference—the root is the same. To rail against politicians for reacting in fear to acquire and protect resources that they believe we need, yet remain oblivious to our own fears of trying to acquire and protect what we believe we need, only perpetuates fear and untruth. It is not very honest to expect others to live without fear when we are not.

To live without fear, however, does not mean that we need to minimize or get rid of what we own. As I gradually realized, it is actually not material possessions that are at the root of the fear created by the belief in ownership. But as was the case with me, life sometimes uses fear around material possessions to bring us to a deeper level of honesty and experiential understanding of what is at the root of this fear.

To me, owning a house felt very weighty. It felt full of responsibility with a lot of anxiety around it. So after I left the marriage and rented a very small apartment, there was a relaxation into a space that I did not feel the weight of responsibility for. Living in a rented space felt very different than when I had owned a house.

So a year later when I began to look for a house to buy and fear came up from seemingly out of nowhere, I looked closely at this fear. I realized that part of the fear had to do with the possibility that once I signed the papers that said 'this house is now mine' that I would actually believe it, feel the weight of responsibility for it and then stress would take over.

But I knew fear was not a truthful motivator not to buy a house so in openness, even to the possibility of identification with ownership, I trusted life. I realized what a wonderful opportunity life was now giving me to own without really owning.

So when my offer on a house was accepted and I then learned of some 'flaws' during the inspection, there was no problem when I noticed the old record running. In awareness of my body tightening as thoughts arose listing what 'should' get done right away and what things can be done over time, the tension was quickly seen through and released. There was no problem with these blips of past programming. It all moved through quickly without a conditioned sense of self being created and without me acting on it.

And then a week or so after the inspection when I got a call from the storage unit I was renting to tell me it was broken into there was only pure openness. As I listened to the woman tell me that the police had been there and they weren't sure if anything had been taken the words passed through freely as if nothing was happening. I was amazed to see that it was truly a nonissue that the storage unit had been broken into and that stuff may have been taken.

When I got to the storage unit, the first thing I saw was some of my books that had been dropped onto the floor. *Talks with Ramana Maharshi, A New Earth* by Tolle and several others had fallen out of a box that had been cut open and left on its side. There were several other boxes and a plastic bag marked 'Easter and Halloween' that were ripped open but the bunny ears and all else seemed to still be there, and Tolle was none worse for the wear.

As I contemplated all of this, I realized that as I listened to the words of the woman from the storage unit tell me that she wasn't sure if stuff had been taken, it was as if there was no one there attached to anything—and not just the possessions—but my body. The sense that there was a body that I owned, was personally responsible for and needed to make sure was comfortable and safe with all these things that could keep it comfortable and safe was not there.

The realization of 'owning without owning' deepened from only possessions to the body.

I realized that someone with very little material possessions can still live in fear, and the wealthy with a lot of possessions can be free of fear.

To really be free of fear involves being free of the feeling of any personal responsibility of ownership for everything—even of our body. If we feel that we are a separate individual who personally owns or possesses even just a body, fear will hound us.

What we feel we own is felt to be personal and what is felt to be personal is felt to be separate from others and life, and then fear seems warranted.

But when nothing is experienced as personal then nothing is felt to be separate and fear falls away.

So regardless of how much money, if any, we have in the bank and how many material possessions we own, each one of us is invited to the deeper surrender of 'owning without owning'.

Chapter 33

Freedom—Beyond Morality

Beyond the realms of right and wrong there is a field.
I will meet you there.
—Rumi

Some become concerned that if all beliefs are seen as mere concepts which cannot be relied on as truth then their sense of morality will be lost, and they and others won't know how to keep behavior in check. But even though most humans consider themself moral and have many beliefs about how to keep behavior in check, we have to admit that we haven't yet been able to live very peacefully together—or with ourself.

Einstein's statement, "A problem cannot be solved at the same level of consciousness in which it was created," points to the truth that there is another way of living together but it is not at the current collective level of consciousness.

'Solutions' that come from the same foundation on which the problem is created never quite work very well.

When we take ourself as flawed and separate it then follows that we believe others are flawed and separate, and it then seems valid to create a society around laws based on making sure we treat others as we want to be treated, as well as punishments when those laws are broken. When we don't trust ourself we cannot trust others or life. But at this level, the factors that determine who the others are that are to be treated as we want to be treated, as well as how that behavior will look, are all very subjective.

We are all conditioned to have certain beliefs of right and wrong, and the beliefs we have are largely dependent on the time and location of our birth. The period of time in which we are born and the location of our birth largely dictate what we come to believe. These beliefs vary widely and are subject to change because they are formed within the boundaries of time and space.

There was a time when many white people believed that black people are inferior and that there should therefore be laws sanctioning the oppression of them. Even many elected officials and religious leaders fervently believed and openly expressed that it is morally okay to discriminate against black people. Some political systems, religions and cultures still have this belief of females and those who are homosexual, and some people in all cultures don't believe it immoral to abuse animals or treat children in a way they wouldn't want to be treated. And most, if not all, societies have the belief that to 'treat others as you want to be treated' only applies to those who have not been caught breaking any laws. For those caught, a system of punishment without the 'treat others as you want to be treated' belief is put into place.

This level of morality comes from fear, not true understanding, so it only serves to perpetuate fear.

There is most definitely another way of being in this world, however, that comes from a completely different foundation than the foundation of fear. This is what Einstein pointed to—a level of consciousness, beyond the boundary of time and space, that directly knows reality as whole and unified. At this level of consciousness, fear does not motivate actions and a completely different level of relating opens.

Chapter 34

The Pursuit of Happiness or the Discovery of Happiness?

The Spanish film *No,* which is about the 1988 election campaign to oust Chilean dictator Pinochet, not only clearly and amusingly demonstrates the universal drive for happiness but also includes a profound scene inadvertently pointing to the futility of trying to externally work toward what each of us individually believes will bring peace or happiness.

The scene is set in slow motion with policemen beating protestors and then the movement stops as a circle is drawn around one policeman and the narrator says, "This man wants peace." The beating continues in slow motion and then the movement stops and a circle is drawn around a protestor being beaten and the narrator says, "This man wants peace." The scene of the protestors being beaten continues to alternate between slow motion and fixed frame as a circle is drawn around a policeman and the narrator says, "This man fights for what he believes," and then the circle is drawn around a protestor and the narrator says, "This man fights for what he believes."

The beating continues as the narrator says, "They have the right to live in peace and have the right to work for what they believe in. Our nation will be great when no Chilean is afraid of another Chilean and when everyone has a place in the homeland."

Although those words may initially sound reasonable and

hopeful, when we consider them a bit more deeply we can directly see the inconsistency and untruth. Both the policemen and the protestors want peace and fight for peace, and both believe that what they are doing is necessary for peace, all of which demonstrates the futility of working for peace at the level of what each of us believe.

If we truly believe happiness or peace is linked to something external then peace is not possible.

The pursuit of peace externally does not allow peace because all kinds of deeply unconscious acts are acted out in that pursuit. How can they not be when we truly believe that something external needs to change—at the same time others believe it doesn't need to be changed or they believe something else needs to be changed?

If we believe that our partner or children or anyone need to be a certain way for us to be happy, we will be motivated by fear to try and change them so that fear is then projected either emotionally or physically or both. We will say and do all sorts of things to try and secure our happiness regardless of how unhappy and afraid those attempts make others. In order for us to one day hopefully live in peace, we do not allow them to live in peace.

If we deeply believe that our happiness and peace are linked to how physically safe we believe we are from being harmed by those of other countries who hate us we will try to ensure our safety by whatever means necessary, even if it involves invading others' privacy or torturing and killing them in the process. In order for us to one day hopefully live in peace, we actually believe that non-peaceful or aggressive methods will get us there.

This drive for peace and happiness is natural, but it can be very destructive and it is always counterproductive when it moves outward. Even the most brutal dictators deeply deluded by ignorance are seeking peace and happiness. When we believe peace is caused by something external, conflict and violence are inevitable—between family members and between countries.

At the level of belief, the religious fundamentalist bombs the abortion clinic or becomes a suicide bomber, and the political fundamentalist destroys government property or invades other countries—all in the name of working toward what they believe is right. The religious fundamentalist calls those who disagree with their religious beliefs sinners or infidels, and the political fundamentalist calls those who disagree with their political beliefs, even those within their own political party, unpatriotic or unenlightened.

But when the religious go within and discover God or Love directly, it is not possible to spread fear and hate. And when those that are politically involved go within and discover Peace or Happiness directly, it is not possible to spread fear and hate. The 'religious' and the 'politically involved' are then speaking the same language and are both moving from love. Clarity and love move very differently than fear and hate, as the movements of Gandhi, Martin Luther King and Nelson Mandela demonstrated.

Although the founders of the United States meant well when they wrote, "We hold these truths to be self-evident, that all Men are created equal, that they are endowed by their Creator with certain unalienable rights, that among these are Life, Liberty and the Pursuit of Happiness," when we contemplate our own experience of pursuing happiness we have to admit that that relentless pursuit for something in the future does not allow us to live in peace now with those we believe are somehow linked to our happiness. The discovery of happiness, however, does. The discovery of happiness is Self-evident—not the pursuit of happiness. The pursuit of happiness is Self-denying.

When we are in pursuit of peace and happiness we work toward some concept that we believe in, which is another way to say that we are working toward what we believe is now lacking, so we are then locked into moving from fear—and fear can only perpetuate fear. But when we go within, beyond or prior to any belief, and experientially, directly discover happiness we are then free to move from this direct experience of truth—and the possibilities of what will arise from that are infinite.

What will the world look like when more humans are no longer seeking peace and happiness because they have already discovered it? When we are no longer using each other to try and find fulfillment because we already know fulfillment—how will that world look?

Let's all first discover what our own world looks like when we directly know and move from love, and then we'll enjoy finding out together what the collective world looks like.

Chapter 35

Waking Up From the Dream of Lack and Separation

If we have a night dream that other people are out to get us, we feel that one dream character is personal, the other dream characters and world are separate and that the dreamer is nonexistent. Within the dream it feels as if we are truly in danger of being hurt because we are not conscious of the consciousness in which the dream is arising, and that the other characters in the dream are not separate. With identification with one dream character fear is experienced because we truly feel that our sense of well-being is dependent on what others do.

But in lucid night dreaming, we are conscious of the reality of the dream and dreamer. Although our awareness may be intermittent, with each glimpse of reality there is a break in fear. The non-personal reality of the one dream character, the non-separate reality of not only the other dream characters but of the whole dream and the true reality of the dreamer are all glimpsed simultaneously. We go from feeling that fear is warranted to glimpsing the reality that who we are is not at all threatened.

And when we wake up completely from the night dream and see all the way through its lingering effects, the full reality is realized without any more forgetfulness. All fear from the perceived dream threats dissolves fully as the totality is realized. Nothing in the dream is believed or felt to be personal or separate from the consciousness in which it all appears.

This is the opportunity each one of us now has in the waking state—to wake up out of the misperception of all that seems so personal or separate. But just as the personal seeming dream character does not wake up to realize itself as the consciousness dreaming, so it is within the waking state. There is never a person that wakes up because there is never an actual separate individual. We don't wake up out of being a person, we wake up out of believing we ever were a person or that which is separate. Lack and separation do not somehow evolve into wholeness—it is realized there never is lack or separation.

Before the realization we believe we are lacking and separate, and then after the realization most of us go through a period where we know we are whole yet often still feel separate. But as fear is directly seen and experienced through, this misperception clears up. We gradually realize that there are not separate whole consciousnesses but that the unified whole is now expressing itself as whatever is taking shape. There is always only Consciousness either misperceiving itself to be one person within the totality or being itself knowingly as the totality.

Although Consciousness expresses itself uniquely in, through and as each form, when we know who we are this unique expression is no longer taken personally. That which expresses itself now as the oak tree and willow tree, the worker ant and the queen ant, the human on death row and the human running the company is one. When oneness is directly known the optical illusion of separation continues but we are no longer deluded by it as the feelings of lack and fear fall away.

Unlike when we wake up out of the night dream and all form

within the dream dissolves completely, this is not the case when we wake up out of the dream of lack and separation in the waking state. When we realize the truth of our being, the play of form or the relative level of experience does not dissolve but the sense of separation and fear does. The dance or play of form continues with all these seemingly separate characters either dancing unconsciously to the beat of the flawed imagined sense of self or dancing consciously to the beat of the whole. The feel of dancing in alignment with or as truth is very different than the feel of dancing in resistance, but we know directly that it is Consciousness dancing it all.

The teaching, within most if not all religions, that states that the Divine is omnipresent is the full truth of it. But this is not something to be believed in but to be discovered and consciously lived.

Chapter 36

Beware of the 'Awake Me'

For many there is such peace and joy when it is realized that the internal nag complaining that something is wrong or missing is not true that there is often a sharing of this joy before it is matured and integrated. And then when synchronistic events or even mystical experiences take place there is a danger of interpreting them to be happening to an awake individual, and share all of that from the standpoint of an 'awake person'. All of this contributes to the creating of an inflated and therefore separate sense of self—albeit an 'awakened one'. Life, however, always moves to dissolve the separate sense of self, even the awakened separate sense of self, not to solidify it. So thankfully, when we share and move from this inflated sense of an awake me life has a tailor-made way of pointing us back to reality.

There was such joy when I realized that what we truly are is not flawed that I could not help but sometimes share this with those close to me. Although I now see that the understanding at that time wasn't yet mature for a certain period of time it felt as if it was, so I ended up sharing with a few close to me the wonderful news that we are not what our thoughts tell us we are. And then some synchronistic events took place that I interpreted to be happening to an 'awake person' which I also shared with some people, and then it all came crashing down—thankfully.

All of this unfolded around a stray cat my then-husband and I took in. This cat was living in the drainage ditch by our house and the way I interpreted the synchronistic circumstances around which Leo came to be a part of our household created an inflated sense of an awake self. And because that was all unconscious I then shared those synchronistic events from the viewpoint of an 'awake person'. Then my husband and I, Leo and our two other cats were on vacation and Leo ran away in that unfamiliar place. Although there was a level of acceptance around his leaving there was also some feeling that I did something wrong. And then when we were back home, quite a few other synchronistic events occurred and he was found and came back to our household and that's when the sense of an awake person really solidified. I felt like all this was happening to a 'me'. There was an awake me, and Life was being good to this awake me. There was such an inflation of joy which I then also shared with some people from the standpoint of an 'awake person'—and then it all came to an abrupt end.

After some time it became clear that Leo could not be in our house with our other two cats so we had to give him up. And simultaneously with the acceptance of giving him up, there was a humility and deepening that took hold. I became very quiet about what was unfolding within and there was a deepening openness to only What Is as I realized that what is has no inflated sense about it.

This dissolving of the personal sense of self involves not only the negative sense of self and the positive sense of self but also the awakened sense of self. The sense of an individual, separate consciousness waking up is a misperception of reality. It is a misperception because it is taking the view that there are separate consciousnesses that wake up and now realize themselves as separate whole consciousnesses.

This view of a separate consciousness that is now awake at some level feels not only separate from life but also separate from others. This 'awake positive me' will always eventually seem as if it is unawake or not awake enough, or will feel some specialness and therefore separateness. Knowing ourself as Universal Consciousness or the unified whole manifesting and expressing itself uniquely within, through and as form has no sense of specialness about it.

There is never a separate person who wakes up because there is never anything separate—but this experiential understanding may take hold gradually. The stage of feeling like a separate individual who is now awake may be a necessary stage most of us go through but it is important not to get stuck there. And simply being aware of this inflated sense of an awake me dissolves it. If, however, there is attachment to this special sense of being an awake me then the unfolding will be delayed, and suffering and confusion will continue. But for those who are completely tired of the false separate sense of self then there is openness to life now which is always in service to the dissolving of all remnants of the inflated sense of self.

The deepening unfolds as we simply remain open to what is—and what is has no personal or separate or inflated sense about it. Whenever any positive or special awakened sense of self rears its head, expose it fully and remain free. It is as simple and direct as that.

Chapter 37

Why It's Necessary That the Personal Self Seem So Convincing

Cause and effect at the relative level help to create a very convincing personal sense of self—when we identify with thought. When a thought is experienced we assume it is true so we believe it, which then causes emotions based on those beliefs, which then cause reactions according to those emotions, which then cause others to react in response to our actions. And since life and the actions of others often reflect back exactly what we believe, the created personal sense of self seems very convincing. It is a kind of closed circuit experience that has just enough consistency to keep us hooked into it for quite some time.

But although it all seems personally self-verifying, there is thankfully a fail-safe glitch lovingly built into it all.

The entire personal sense of self is created on the assumption that our thoughts are true which then creates the impression that thoughts come from an actual solid personal separate self. We are so convinced our thoughts come from a separate self because we assume no one else is having our thoughts and that our thoughts are giving us a factual account of what our senses seem to be perceiving as the external world of separate, independent objects.

When we misperceive thoughts as personal then the mind or consciousness and the body or senses are also misperceived, and then from that faulty foundation they work together to form what seems to be the only perspective of experience—internal, personal thoughts and external, independent objects. But if we consider experience from a more unified whole perspective we see that the personal separate self is not the only perspective.

Each wave in the ocean has different content floating around in it. One wave may have some seaweed and fish, the wave next to it some sand and bubbles, and the next wave some bubbles and fish and then the content may switch or some new content may come in. Just because each wave has different content or content that is unknown by another wave does not mean the waves are separate and that the content is personal. And because each wave looks out into the same ocean and sees the same (or different) content within the ocean, it does not mean that the ocean is separate or even that the objects are separate and independent of the ocean and waves. The water itself may in fact be an alive, intelligent energy now manifesting as whatever form is within it. To assume otherwise is simply that—an assumption. But it is an assumption that may actually have some very definite consequences because the intelligent energy may also be a loving energy which allows the waves to experience whatever they now choose—life as what feels like a separate independent wave, or life as the wave actually is. The choice between what is and what is assumed about what is may actually be the choice between heaven and hell.

The perspective of a separate personal self does not hold up as the only perspective when considered in this light. Of course none of this proves the absence of separation but it does show that separation is not the only perspective. Given the current limitations of science, some may argue that separation is the only rational perspective, but there is a glitch built into the separate sense of self which does expose it as undeniably false—but by honest, direct experience not by analyzing experience based on the preconception of separation.

There is an inconsistency to the personal sense of self that eventually brings about a malfunction of sorts. Thankfully, that which is untrue lacks integrated consistency and this lack of integrity does not feel harmonious to the truth of who we are.

When we assume thoughts are true we then feel as if they come from a personal self so we understandably think that we wouldn't lie to ourself so we, without question, then believe we are who we think we are. But when we stop for a moment and look dispassionately at our thoughts, we see such inconsistency and untruth in them which then opens the possibility to investigate that maybe we are in fact not what our thoughts tell us we are.

Obsessively, thoughts tell us that in order for us to be happy or at peace we need something additional than what is now, but even when we get what our thoughts tell us we need and then peace leaves we unquestioningly continue to pursue whatever our thoughts tell us next. Why do we continue to fall for that? Why do we continue to believe our thoughts even though some prove to be outright lies or change so easily from one judgment to the opposite judgment, and we believe each one equally without hesitation? But then at other times we believe one thought but not another—why is that? If thoughts really come from a separate self, why can't we control our thoughts so that we have all positive thoughts or at least have thoughts that are consistent? Why when others' actions or life reflect back our beliefs we are quick to say, "See I knew he didn't like me," or "I knew life was out to get me," but when they don't reflect back our beliefs we do not question those beliefs? We can think one thing, say another thing and then do the exact opposite. During a discussion about the state of the world, we can have a thought about eating mushroom pizza, then say we want to live in peace and then in the next breath yell at our children for yelling at each other. It's a wonder why we don't stop and say, "Yeah, wait a minute! What's going on here?" But we don't even consider looking at any of this because we think that to question our thoughts we are questioning our existence.

Eventually, however, the inconsistent nature of the personal sense of self brings about such a level of dissatisfaction that we can no longer run from it. There are not enough TV programs or things to do or substances to ingest to distract or numb us so we come to a place where we have to find out the truth.

The human dimension is a call Home to what we never really left because it is impossible to leave home when home is universal or the totality of all that is. But how could we ever recognize the unified whole when there is nothing outside of it? Since there is nothing outside of it, it would be impossible for us to be conscious of that which is universal—unless we could somehow misperceive it all.

Within this human experience, how else could we ever consciously know Universal Consciousness unless we could misperceive it as a personal, separate consciousness, feel the inconsistency and unnatural limitations of that as untrue and then consciously sense what is true? And how could we ever misperceive Universal Consciousness or that which is formless as personal or separate unless Consciousness appears as innocent relative, temporary form—along with the fluidity of Consciousness within the waking state to identify with form and misperceive it all? And in order to misperceive form as personal or separate there has to be enough hook to that misperception. There has to be just enough consistency to the misperception but also just enough inconsistency which results in a sufficient amount of confusion and dissatisfaction in order to point the way out.

The Absolute within and as the relative as it actually is feels very different than when there is a personal seeming overlay to the relative.

Life is pure loving Intelligence. There are no mistakes.

What joy there is when we come Home after 'being away'. What love is revealed when the innocent misperception is seen through and reality is realized.

The directly-known consistency or integrity of Life registers as a full harmony of being at the levels of our understanding, sensing and expressing.

The inconsistent personal seeming cause and effect that solidifies the personal sense of self is over, as well as the completely consistent cause and effect during the process of awakening that serves to dissolve the remnants of the personal as well as the inflated awakened sense of self.

Without the confusion and dissatisfaction created by the

inconsistency of cause and effect we would not seek the truth of who we are. And after the realization of who we are, without the consistency of cause and effect the clear discrimination between what is directly known to be true and what is believed to be true would not unfold. Thankfully, when we believe we are the inconsistent or changeful one then cause and effect is inconsistent in confirming that false identity so we feel as if something is lacking. And when we realize ourself as the consistent or ever-present one then cause and effect is fully consistent in confirming our true nature and we sense directly nothing is lacking.

When the closed circuit experience of the personal seeming self is over as well as the limited sense of experience within the dissolving of all residual impressions of the personal as well as awakened separate sense of self—then the dance of life is free to reveal itself as outside of any preconception.

Anything is now possible—even peace on earth.

What joy we will now have together as we explore and celebrate life as it actually is.

Chapter 38

The Dance

There is a dance you are dancing
do you feel the music?

When you lean into it
it takes hold of every cell
and swings them this way and that
to the steady beat
that is the ground and the sky and everything in between.

It all rocks
to the same
constant,
relentlessly
Loving
beat.

You know you're going to dance it
all the way through
so why not
dance it
with full, unfettered abandon?

Lose the timidity,
let the arms swing.

Drop all caution,
let the legs jump.

Who said the dance should look a certain way?
Don't believe a word of it.
Feel the beat
Now

And lose
and find
yourself
in it—

and then all bets are off
as
the Infinite's Dance of Celebration
moves.

If you have enjoyed this book, why not tell other readers by posting a review on your preferred booksite?

Recent bestsellers from O-Books are:

Heart of Tantric Sex

Diana Richardson

Revealing Eastern secrets of deep love and intimacy to Western couples.

Paperback: 978-1-90381-637-0

e-book: 978-1-84694-637-0

Crystal Prescriptions

The A-Z guide to over 1,200 symptoms and their healing crystals

Judy Hall

The first in the popular series of four books, this handy little guide is packed as tight as a pill-bottle with crystal remedies for ailments.

Paperback: 978-1-90504-740-6

e-book: 978-1-84694-629-5

Take Me To Truth

Undoing the Ego

Nouk Sanchez, Tomas Vieira

The best-selling step-by-step book on shedding the Ego, using the teachings of A Course In Miracles.

Paperback: 978-1-84694-050-7

e-book: 978-1-84694-654-7

7 Myths about Love...Actually!

The The journey from your HEAD to the HEART of your SOUL

Mike George

Smashes all the myths about LOVE.

Paperback: 978-1-84694-288-4

e-book: 978-1-84694-682-0

The Holy Spirit's Interpretation of the New Testament

A course in Understanding and Acceptance

Regina Dawn Akers

Following on from the strength of A Course in Miracles, NTI teaches us how to experience the love and oneness of God.

Paperback: 978-1-84694-085-9

e-book: 978-1-78099-083-5

The Message of A Course In Miracles

A translation of the text in plain language

Elizabeth A. Cronkhite

A translation of A Course in Miracles into plain, everyday language for anyone seeking inner peace. The companion volume, Practicing a Course In Miracles, offers practical lessons and mentoring.

Paperback: 978-1-84694-319-5

e-book: 978-1-84694-642-4

Rising in Love

My Wild and Crazy Ride to Here and Now, with Amma, the Hugging Saint

Ram Das Batchelder

Rising in Love conveys an author's extraordinary journey of spiritual awakening with the Guru, Amma.

Paperback: 978-1-78279-687-9

e-book: 978-1-78279-686-2

Thinker's Guide to God

Peter Vardy

An introduction to key issues in the philosophy of religion.

Paperback: 978-1-90381-622-6

Your Simple Path

Find happiness in every step

Ian Tucker

A guide to helping us reconnect with what is really important in our lives.

Paperback: 978-1-78279-349-6

e-book: 978-1-78279-348-9